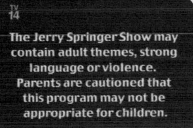

TV
14

The Jerry Springer Show may
contain adult themes, strong
language or violence.
Parents are cautioned that
this program may not be
appropriate for children.

JERRY Springer's

Wildest Shows Ever!

INTRODUCTION BY JERRY SPRINGER

EDITED BY RICHARD DOMINICK, EXECUTIVE PRODUCER OF THE *JERRY SPRINGER SHOW*

CADER BOOKS

STUDIOS
USA

HarperEntertainment
A Division of HarperCollinsPublishers

FIRST EDITION

Designed by Charles Kreloff

Produced by Cader Books
38 E. 29 Street
New York, NY 10016

Library of Congress Cataloging-in-Publication Data is available.

ISBN 0-06-107361-X

96 97 98 99 00   10 9 8 7 6 5 4 3 2 1

Contents

JERRY *Springer*

DO YOU HATE SOMEONE BECAUSE THEY'RE TRYING TO STEAL YOUR LOVER? DO YOU WANT TO CONFRONT THEM ON OUR SHOW?

Introduction

This show is a fun, crazy circus. My job is to bring on the acts: either outrageous people, or normal people caught up in outrageous situations. The concept is really the same as the old *Ed Sullivan Show*—although he would probably turn over in his grave at the comparison. Like Ed, I just say, "And the next act..."

I look at it as the greatest job in the world. I love it. Every day I meet incredibly interesting people. I get to be right in the middle of this circus—okay, occasionally I have to catch a flying chair—and people treat me incredibly well. Sometimes people will say, "Oh, poor you," and I say, "You don't really mean that, because you would take this job in a second." This is camp. Basically, I get paid to go to camp.

Jerry, from his very first show, on September 30, 1991.

It's easy to understand why I love it. But why do so many other people? I believe it's because other folks are not used to seeing this craziness on television. We know it exists in life. But mainstream television has historically offered only a white, upper-middle-class perspective. There's nothing wrong with a white, upper-middle-class perspective, but it's wrong when that's the only perspective. American television is at its best when it reflects the entire culture, not simply one group.

Let's face it, most television programming is plastic. Every news anchor is a clone of every other; everything is so canned. Suddenly, our show comes along and you see people you've never seen on television before. It's shocking. To hear what people are doing, even the profanity they use. It's not like we don't know it exists, but we can't believe it's on television! Finally, here is something that isn't a cliche.

There's so much posturing out there that it's almost

JERRY *Springer*

ARE YOU PREGNANT AND WORKING IN THE SEX INDUSTRY?

refreshing to see people just being real. We don't give people a script or tell them to say things in a certain sanitized way; we let them be as they truly are at that moment. My guests are not afraid to say what they're thinking. Perhaps we are the real politically incorrect show. And people love that. It's like when you were in school, and you knew it was inappropriate when some kid yelled out to the teacher, but there was an excitement there because the kid was saying what everyone else was thinking but just didn't have the guts to say.

Jerry with his first panel of guests, also from September 30, 1991.

Now, as for the language—think about it. If you just found out from your college roommate that he was sleeping with your girlfriend, you wouldn't say, "Bob, that is inappropriate." You would say exactly what people on our show say—and pretty much the way they say it. To see someone having that kind of an honest reaction is the magic of the show.

Who is our audience? Mainstream America. Average people who are not necessarily outrageous themselves. Go to any corporate office building and hang around the watercooler. People will talk about the episode they watched the night before. This may be what angers our critics most—that Middle America seems to love it.

My role is to play the normal guy, the average Joe. I ask questions or make wise-cracks just like the viewer does. I say what I would say if I was sitting at home with a bunch of guys watching this craziness. Anybody could do what I do; a dolt could do what I do. And I am proud to be that dolt.

I think my main job is to stay out of the way. I believe that the greatest baseball announcers are the ones who know when to keep their mouths shut and let the moment speak for itself. Let's be honest. No one is tuning in to look at Jerry Springer. If you see me in an episode a lot , you know it's not working. It's dying and I'm trying to pull something out of the guests. If there's something great happening onstage, they don't need me. The show is definitely at its best when there's a lot of passionate action and I can stay back in the audience and simply watch.

Part of what makes the show work—I can say with absolutely clear hindsight—is that I don't belong there. I dress differently than most of my guests, I talk differently. That helps to give the show its edge. It's the same feeling you would get, to use that school analogy again, if your parents were visiting your class on a day that everything got out of hand. Part of the thrill would be wondering how they were going to react to all that craziness.

JERRY Springer

DOES SOMEONE IN YOUR LIFE CONSTANTLY INTERFERE IN YOUR RELATIONSHIPS AND YOU WANT TO TELL THEM TO BACK OFF?

I prepare for the show only slightly more than the typical audience member prepares for it. That is to say, I don't want to know much of anything beforehand. If I know what is going to happen, I might doze off and think about something else. This way, I'm more on edge.

One thing I can say: I love my guests. They're just naturally good, salt-of-the-earth people—who happen to use colorful language. Obviously there are individuals I don't like, such as the Klan people—but most of our guests are generally good folks who are simply passionate about something at the moment.

I never try to be disrespectful to the people on stage. I'll have fun with them, but I know that I'm not better than they are. They may be more pissed off because they just got dumped, but they react the way most people would react. And I love how in the middle of a show someone who is all riled up and cursing the bluest language can suddenly turn to me and cheerfully say, "Oh, hi, Jerry!" To be honest, I'm more comfortable around these people than I am around executives. In fact, this is the very same constituency I had in politics, when I was a city councilman and, later, mayor of Cincinnati: the young, minorities, blue-collar people, liberals, the college crowd, the disenfranchised. Nothing has changed.

The thing I always tell other people is that this show is not about anything very serious most of the time—it's about who's dating whom, who's dumping whom. The world will easily go on well without the show, just as it is now surviving okay with it. In fact, I don't know why they even call this a talk show—hardly anybody does any talking! The same can be said of our book. It's not serious literature; it's a whole variety of our strangest, wildest, most provocative, and most unexpected shows and moments. So enjoy this book the same way you enjoy our show. And remember, till next time, take care of yourself and each other.

—JERRY SPRINGER

Welcome to the Show

It's safe to say that in the history of television, no show has ever been like the *Jerry Springer Show*. Food fights among feuding family members. Wives ripping hair off their husbands' mistresses' heads. Epic battles between men and their lovers' secret boyfriends. A Christmas celebrated Ku Klux Klan style. Even a guy who married his horse!

But when you get right down to it, it's amazing that there hasn't been. The concept of the *Jerry Springer Show* is so breathtakingly simple: Let real people reveal their raw and uncensored anger, joy, and secret lifestyles before an eager audience. In the annals of television, it has always been the most unadorned ideas that have succeeded. After all, *Wheel of Fortune* is just hangman, *Jeopardy!* is a big Q&A, and *The Price Is Right* is pumped-up shopping. *Jerry Springer* is the modern day backyard fence over which we can marvel at other peoples' hidden words and deeds.

Sure, there have always been soap-opera actors baring incest and infidelities, but everyone knows they're just reading their lines. And celebrities regularly confess their numerous sexual dalliances and childhood terrors, but most viewers can't relate to their lifestyles. The *Jerry Springer Show* has struck a chord because it puts regular people—such as a man, his wife, and his mistress—onstage together and stands back while the inevitable wildness follows. Ironically, for a show that reveals outrageous secrets to friends and lovers, this show flourishes because nothing is out of view. What the audience sees is everything there is.

It's the Guests, Stupid

This show is all about the guests' lives, unusual though some of them may be. The *Jerry Springer Show* simply gives guests a forum in which to portray that life, and the audience is welcome to peek. No guest is blindsided or ambushed on our program; the game works only because everyone has agreed to the roll of the dice, regardless of its outcome. Jerry is the sympathetic host; he never judges or condemns the guests for their behavior (although the studio audience certainly weighs in with its opinions).

The guests are everything to this show. Without their truthfulness and honest reactions the show wouldn't succeed. An ideal guest is one filled with passion; someone who is energetic, involved in the story, cares about its out-

JERRY *Springer*

ARE YOU A WOMAN ACCUSED OF STALKING A MAN AND YOU WANT TO CONFRONT HIM ON OUR SHOW?

come, and explodes like a firecracker when the cameras turn on. Guests who yell, scream, cry, jump out of their seats, pull hair, and yes, throw an occasional punch in what has become the Super Bowl of confrontations. Like the wife who got wind that her two-timing bisexual husband had called the show, and immediately phoned associate producer Toby Yoshimura to shout into the phone line, "I need a plane ticket! I want to confront this bastard!" (As expected, this woman was a bursting comet when she subsequently appeared onstage and the episode was a smash hit.) Or like the men who fess up to everything—Yes, I'm sleeping with this one and with that one, and I'm going to keep doing it—instead of offering half-hearted denials.

Our producers have honed their radar to the point where they can usually spot a passionate guest on the telephone seconds after they say hello. But we don't hear it often. The person who initially calls the program is nearly always bursting to get their story out, but the other people involved in the relationship are frequently more reticent. Yet the show will not go on the air without them. What largely sets the *Jerry Springer Show* apart from most other talk shows is our insistence that all the key players in the relationship must participate.

So who are these guests? They are average Americans, flying in from Boston, Seattle, Dallas, New York, and everywhere in between. Certainly, most are not wealthy, but then neither are the vast majority of people in this country. For the most part, they are normal people having normal relationship problems; the only difference is that they agree to share their problems with the world, while most of us won't even confess our anguish to our dearest friends. These may not be the kinds of people you are used to seeing on television, but that doesn't mean there's anything unreal about them. Our feeling is that we are one of the first shows to depict real Americans, every day, in all their quirky glory. And in doing so, we touch so many people who have long been disenfranchised on television.

Watching Without Sound

When I first took over the show in 1994, one of the first things I did was to put a sign on my door giving a directive to the show's producers. It read in effect, "Bring it to me with the sound off." At the time, the show was an also-ran talking-heads talk show, with Jerry in the prepackaged role of the next Phil Donahue. The program was inches from cancellation.

Not many talk shows at the time were looking for a show that made sense without sound, but why not? Human nature dictates that people crave action. I remembered the rush I got as a five-year-old boy watching my beloved wrestling matches, with the energized crowd shrieking at the colorful characters and their outrageous antics until everyone's throats went hoarse. I knew that television had the power to make all of us that five-year-old boy again. But instead, the medium was putting out the most boring entertainment in the world, shows featuring a bunch of people talking and the audience sitting with their hands in their laps.

I felt sure we could harness the real power of television with our focus on passionate guests. For with passion comes action—and action can be watched without sound. The reactions of the studio audience are our barometer for how well we are succeeding. If the people spontaneously jump to their feet, chanting "Jerry! Jerry!" throughout a segment, the episode is a winner. When the crowd is absorbed by the wild, outrageous, and often shocking drama unfolding before them, how can the viewer at home not be? The goal is to give people a rise, and keep them craving more. As long as we're booked two months in advance to get in the studio, we know we're hot. There are some talk shows that send buses around to fill up their audience. Not us. People want to come to our show. It's an unforgettable experience.

What You Want to Watch

This show is produced for the enjoyment of our viewers, pure and simple. When an episode attracts a large audience, we've done our job. We hear from our fans frequently and often: they say they love the show and they don't want us to change it. Of course the things that get a rise out of the audience change with the times, and the show does shift direction to stay in tune with our viewership. In the early days, sex was often the vehicle that aroused the crowd. The crowd was amazed by the sight of women who secretly yearned to be strippers, or porn stars who took it all off onstage, or people who simply refused to be constrained by clothes. In recent years, as viewers have grown immune to sex, the show has moved more toward relationship issues, which pack a different kind of wallop. It doesn't get much better than the episode "You Stole My Lover!" featured in this book, in which two women battle it out so ferociously for their shared man that one yanks the braided wig off the other's head. Or when the boyfriend in "Surprise…I'm a Transsexual" (also featured) confesses to his startled sex partner that he is really a woman. Even today, though, not all the shows are about romances. Occasionally a curveball is thrown to shake things up a bit and keep the viewers from becoming complacent. Some of the best of these shows are also profiled in this book, including the ever-popular "Jerry Rescues an Obese Man" and the saga of the New York City tunnel-dwellers, "The Mole People."

What's Next?

The truth is that the show has never followed a master plan, and that is part of what makes it continue to work so well. Most of the best elements simply evolve in a natural flow. Switching from sex to relationships happened when it seemed like it was time for a change. The addition of Steve Wilkos and his fellow security guards came about when a Klan show was planned and we feared that things might get

ARE YOU CHEATING ON YOUR LOVER AND YOU FEEL IT'S TIME TO CONFESS?

out of hand. No one expected the men to later become celebrities in their own right.

So where the show will evolve next is anybody's guess. But no topic is off limits. Every corner of society—no matter how revolting others may find it—deserves a forum on TV, and we're here to provide it. If Huntsville, Texas, told us that Henry Lee Lucas could be executed on the *Jerry Springer Show*, we would have our cameras rolling that afternoon. Though Jerry's relatives were killed in the Holocaust, we still give neo-Nazis their moment. Nobody has the right to censor people from the airwaves. Plus, it's good to let them go up there and spout all their nonsense and let the audience see how stupid they are; giving light to their toxic views is the best way to disinfect them.

Though some people say our show is over the top, each episode is really a tidy little morality play. If you pay attention to the audience, you'll notice that they are swift to impose a strong moral sense on the guests, viscerally booing two-timing husbands and hate-spewing KKK members when they tell their tales (or, often, before they even get a chance to speak). The day we do a show and the wife-beater gets applauded is the day we bring down the curtain; that's the end of the world.

The People Backstage

As our fans know, there is no show on television like the *Jerry Springer Show*. Behind the scenes, production assistants, associate producers, and producers work countless, exhausting hours putting this great show together. On any given morning at 3 A.M., the production area buzzes with electricity, excitement, and enthusiasm as the dedicated production team puts everything they have into this show. In the same vein, all of the crazy on-stage antics are meaningless without the director, his staff, and the camera crew skillfully and cleverly catching this outrageousness and bringing into our fans' living rooms. I would like to take this opportunity to praise and applaud the production team and the technical crew for their tireless efforts and ferocious commitment. Without all of these individual efforts, there would be no show.

And Now...the Top Shows

While every *Jerry Springer Show* offers a wild adventure, the memorable episodes handpicked by our staff for this book have everything that makes a show terrific: extreme passion, explosive guests, bizarre and wild actions, and outrageous reactions. Presented in the order in which they aired, each show is covered from beginning to end, chronicling all the action in words and pictures. Behind-the-scenes anecdotes help show you more about how the stories evolve, and help you to understand more about the key players (since a one-hour, action-packed show is often not long enough to get every detail out). But for the most part, we've stuck to the basics of these unforgettable stories, because each show really speaks for itself—the show is the show, as we say. The "I Married a Horse" episode, however, will be new to even the most devoted fan, since it was ultimately deemed too graphic to air. But not, thank goodness, to print. Read on for an exclusive peek at this outrageous show, which features a man conducting a sexual and romantic relationship with his pony—and the two other guests who have their own unique lovers: dogs! Like the audience in the studio, and the viewers at home, hang onto your seats as you turn these pages. We promise you a hell of a ride.

—RICHARD DOMINICK
EXECUTIVE PRODUCER

Be Our Guest

Probably the most frequently asked question about the show is, Where do these people come from? The answer is alarmingly simple: The show receives over 3,000 phone calls a week from people desperate to come and tell their stories.

Springer fans will immediately recognize the questions featured on these introductory pages, which often appear after commercial breaks in the show. These guest searches are the main provocation for those thousands of calls. Those who have never called the program's toll-free number (1-800-96-JERRY) would surely be taken aback by the show's elaborate voice mail system: "Press one if you're really a man living as a woman, press two if you want to confront your husband's mistress..." Each caller is asked to leave a message, and each of these thousands of messages is transcribed (the record is known by program insiders as "carts") and passed along to the program's half-dozen producers and their assistants.

A small number of the program's guests come from Internet searches, especially for touchy topics like incest, or from producers calling local strip clubs and bars. Past guests, too, often offer their friends as leads; one woman who obviously lives in a modern day Peyton Place has provided dozens of sources alone.

Producers and their assistants daily cull through the carts relevant to their niches; some specialize in angry wives or bisexual love triangles, while others traffic in transsexuals or sexy secrets. Everyone who leaves a message of any kind will receive a delicate call back from a *Springer* associate producer (each often logs over a hundred calls a day).

"I telephone every person on the cart, even if the message sounds like a joke, because you just don't know," explains associate producer Toby Yoshimura. "When you get the call, 'I'm sleeping with my grandmother and I'm also married to my cousin and I'm also...' at some point you're pretty sure it's not true." But he can never say never. One call Toby was certain was a fake was from a guy who said his son planned to marry the man's wife; unbelievably, it turned out to be true. In a rousing episode, stepmom and son were soon joined in holy matrimony onstage. And of course, it was Toby who first listened to the incredible message, "I left my wife for a horse," which ultimately became the outlandish episode, "I Married a Horse."

At this point, very little shocks the veteran producers, although a few guests still have the power to startle. Coordinating producer Gina Huerta, for example, was taken aback when a thirtysomething woman told her she was having sex with the seventeen-year-old boy who had deflowered her pre-teen daughter, and when two young sisters claimed they loved getting it on together.

After getting the gist of the story and evaluating the guest for his or her level of passion, the producers next try

JERRY *Springer*

IS YOUR TEENAGER
COMPLETELY OUT OF CONTROL?
DO THEY SAY THEY HATE YOU?
WOULD YOU LIKE
TO CONFRONT THEM
ON OUR SHOW?

to round up the other players. The *Jerry Springer Show* will never book a story unless all the major participants appear. In other words, if you're a cheating dog you have to bring each of your victims with you! But oftentimes one or more key participants can't be located, or is found and refuses to appear, or won't be out of jail in time for the taping.

But because they feature real individuals, even well-planned future shows are held together by a single hair-strand. A willing participant calls back to change his mind. A girl phones her mother about her upcoming appearance and mom forbids her participation. A gal planning to confront her man onstage has it out with him at his office instead. Or a pregnant woman unexpectedly goes into early labor (see "Woman in Labor Confronts Mistress" for one wild episode where such a technicality didn't stop the show). The most fabulously planned show can be lost in minutes. Although the producers try to keep several potential stories in the hopper as backup, staffers have been known to barhop through Chicago until 5 A.M. looking to replace a show lost at the last minute. "I go around to all my bartender friends, asking them who's lonely at the bar and possibly going though a relationship crisis," Toby says. And it has worked.

Prove It or Lose It

Frequently, potential guests don't turn into actual ones because they cannot prove their story, a requirement bordering on the religious at the *Jerry Springer Show*. "We insist on seeing proof for absolutely everything there can be proof for," says senior producer Rachelle Consiglio.

If you say you are married, cough up your marriage license. Known the person since high school? Send over your yearbook. Called the cops against your lover? Get copies of the police report. Claim your mistress is your sibling? Fax over both your birth certificates. Had to get a restraining order against your ex? Send a copy of the court documents. Living together? Bills in both your names, please.

Producers have even become experts at determining if guests have had the sex they claim. While they obviously can't be inside the participants' bedroom, they do pose a long list of detailed questions to each participant: When did you last have sex? What size bed were you on? What color were the sheets? Did you use candles? Any foreign objects? How long did the encounter last? Who watched the kids? Clever producers even put the first caller on hold while they call the other participant(s), ensuring that there will be no collusion.

Guests are also warned that when they get to the show they will be asked to sign an affidavit vouching for the accuracy of everything they say. If they are caught lying, they are told, they will be held liable for the episode's entire produc-

Bringing Them In from Out of Town

Many *Jerry Springer Show* guests come from outside Chicago where the show is taped. Their travel and accommodations alone could provide the plot for an episode:

• One guest missed eight flights in a row when she repeatedly went to the wrong airport or the wrong airline.

• An airport gate agent once tried to keep a transsexual off a flight because her ID was in a man's name.

• Guests cleaned out the entire minibar so often the show has banned them from all rooms.

• One woman stormed the hotel room where the "other woman" was staying, broke down the door, and spent the day in jail.

• A group of strippers refused to stop flashing other patrons in their hotel lobby.

tion cost. That threat is enough to dissuade most any remaining fakers. "After I've given that legal speech to a guest, people have hung up on me," coordinating producer Gina Huerta says. Those who clear through this last hurdle unscathed are soon on their way to the airport—and to the show's studio in Chicago.

What Makes Them Do It?

Why guests not only agree to be on the *Jerry Springer Show* but are practically breaking down the doors to get chosen has become probably the show's next most-asked question, but it is one that is impossible to answer. The reasons are as individual as the guests are, although producers say a few common rationales have emerged.

For some guests, the status quo has been going on forever and simply is no longer working. They need to make a change—and make it stick. "Many guests feel they need an audience when they say these things so either they or the other person will actually believe it," explains associate producer Toby Yoshimura. "Either they have been saying, 'I'm leaving you,' to the person hundreds of times at home, but 15 minutes later they always change their mind. Or they have been trying to confront a person who continually hangs up on them and slams the door in their face. Here, the person will finally have to listen."

Some guests simply want to share their opinions and lifestyles with others. "They want to say, 'This is how I live and I don't care how anybody else reacts to it,'" Toby says. No matter how nasty their beliefs or opinions, people know they can voice them with confidence on the *Jerry Springer Show*.

Some guests also experience a certain satisfying closure after doing a show, almost regardless of its outcome. One man who came on the show hoping to win back his wife, but was unsuccessful, still phoned Toby a few months later to say that the show had been cathartic for him. Even though the wife didn't return to him, having called her new boyfriend every name in the book finally allowed him to move on with his life. It's certainly cheaper than psychotherapy!

Warring parties are booked on separate flights and hosted at separate hotels so as to avoid a pre-show confrontation. These sleeping arrangements create an instant problem for the men bringing both their wives and mistresses: which one to stay with the night before? Often, they will stay with the one they are most afraid will not appear at the taping, even if that person is ultimately not who they will go home with after the show. But while balancing two women might be tough for most of us, these guys have been doing it for months or even years at home!

After the show, most guests say they are thrilled that they did it. They are thankful for the wild ride—even if they have been humiliated by their lover, beaten up by his mistress, and booed by the audience. After all, who doesn't relish those 15 minutes of fame? Weeks and months later producers regularly hear from many of their past guests, offering up the latest twist on their love life and appealing for another shot at the lime-light. In most cases, if they have been great guests and done their jobs well, the producers are only too happy to oblige.

JERRY *Springer*

IS A WOMAN SAYING YOU ARE THE FATHER OF HER CHILD, BUT YOU DON'T BELIEVE HER AND WOULD LIKE A PATERNITY TEST?

Too Hot for Television?

Even a show as racy and risqué as the *Jerry Springer Show* has standards of what it will and will not air. Though it may push the envelope farther than most other programs, the show must still adhere to Federal Communication Commission guidelines and American laws regarding violence, nudity, obscenity, and defamation. We all know from the special videotapes that plenty of what happens in the *Springer* studio is too hot for broadcast television. The interesting question is what is just hot enough, and where is the line drawn? The fascinating and fast-paced job of answering that question falls to the show's onsite attorney, Andrew Savage, a trial lawyer with a strong First Amendment background whose past clients included *Playboy* magazine. Andrew screens each episode, carefully noting the time code of any material he deems must be removed. Savage and executives at the *Jerry Springer Show* are virulent defenders of the First Amendment. But Andrew does confront some rather unusual questions that are not the standard subject of network discussion.

You Can't Say [Bleep]

Long after comedian George Carlin made famous the "seven dirty words," television shows are still prohibited from using these basic terms. Savage has added a few other choice words to his list of unacceptables, which is subject to regular reevaluation. (Some Southern affiliates have argued that "bitch" should also be banned, but so far it is staying.) A small amount of bleeping in an episode can add to the off-color charm of the show. But producers are never happy when guests string them out one after another. "We tell them before the show to please try to watch the swearing, because if they keep doing it no one will hear their story," coordinating producer Gina Huerta explains. "Of course, when their husband's mistress is right in front of them, it's hard not to want to call her every name in the book, and many of them do."

Indefensible

Another area in which the show is very careful is when defamation is an issue. If guests make negative comments about people who are not present to defend themselves, those remarks are generally removed. So while it is OK for a guest to say, "All my aunts are ho's,"—as Donna does in "Holiday Hell with My Feuding Family" (featured in the book)—because all her aunts are on the stage, that same comment would have been bleeped if even one aunt was missing.

It is often for this reason that viewers sometimes know there is more to a story than what they are hearing. "Tell them with whom you cheated on your husband," man-snatching Gina goads her sister Lisa in the outrageous episode, "My Sister Stole My Husband." Lisa never does reveal her secret, but even if she had, it would not have aired, since that party (or parties) was not present at the show.

I've Got a Secret

Another hotspot carefully managed by the show involves the "secrets" programs. Whenever the show features a surprise revelation, guests are required to read, consider, and sign a "secrets list" before they are allowed to appear. The list details 20 possible scenarios, one of which is the actual secret that will be revealed during the program. The show takes every possible precaution, because "we make sure the secret is not going to destroy the people involved," Savage says. This colorful list includes such possibilities as:

Your girlfriend is really a man (interestingly, a lot of guys say they're more worried that their girlfriend is pregnant than that she's a man)
Your boyfriend is really a woman
Your lover/spouse wants to have a threesome
Your lover/spouse is cheating on you
Your lover/spouse works in the sex industry (for example, stripper, prostitute, or porn star)
Your lover/spouse has a sexual fetish

In special circumstances, the list must be expanded to 21 to include the topic of the day. One of the few positive secrets on the list is "Your boyfriend or girlfriend wants to propose," yet somehow, time and again, overly hopeful guests always assume this one is the revelation that awaits them.

The Guys

This may be the *Jerry Springer Show*, but viewers have also been greatly smitten by two other show regulars, security chief Steve Wilkos and stage manager Todd Schultz. These beefy studs can alternately be found breaking up an epic battle or hosting a naked stripper in their lap. Each now gets reams of fan mail from female viewers—which the single Todd and newly divorced Steve happily answer. And let's not forget the rapidly snapped up new bumper sticker, "Steve Saved My Ass!" For all you fawning gals and wanna-be tough guys, here are the men's stories, in their own words:

Steve Wilkos

"I started in May of 1994. I'm a Chicago police officer, and they hired some of us to do security off-duty for a Ku Klux Klan show. We all wore suits and ties and stood around on the sides. I took the job because the pay was pretty decent. At the time, I didn't even know who Jerry Springer was. After that, when they needed security, they started calling me. Soon they said they wanted me all the time.

"I still work as a police officer from 4 P.M. to midnight six days a week. But I have begun considering the *Jerry Springer Show* my real job because it pays well and is more fun, not to mention a lot less dangerous. [The other *Jerry Springer Show* security regulars are fellow police officers Steve recruited for the show: Dave Johnsen, Michael McDermott, Mike O'Connor, Al Perales, and Jimmy Sherlock.]

"I don't consider myself a celebrity; I think of myself as a cop who works on a TV show. But when people see me, they see a TV personality. It can be pretty humorous. For example, the other night I was working as a cop in a rough area of town. My partner goes home early so I am there by myself. It's close to midnight and I see three guys in their car, but when the light turns green they don't go. I beep the horn and they still don't move, so I call for backup and get out of my car. One of the three guys in the car is acting really nervous, so I pull him out and I stick my gun to his ribs because I'm thinking maybe he has a weapon. I tell him, 'If you move, I'm going to shoot you,' and he looks at me and he says, 'Hey, you're Steve from *Jerry Springer*!' So I put the gun away; I know he's not going to shoot me—in fact, he asks for my autograph. Another time when I was called to a house for a domestic dispute, I get there and everybody's screaming and the whole house is torn apart.

All of a sudden they look at me and they smile and say, 'Steve! Can we get tickets to the show?' It's crazy.

"One thing that's interesting is that, as police officers, we all deal every day with the things that are featured on the show. People say, 'This can't be real,' but we cops know it is. On the streets we always see transsexuals, transvestites, strippers, you name it."

"At some point along the way I was asked to travel with Jerry as his security. Jerry would get mobbed wherever he went and I would help protect him. But in the last few seasons as the show has taken off I've become totally useless to him because people mob me also. It's kind of funny. There's a Steve fan club, Steve web sites, those bumper stickers, T-shirts. Women send me gifts, and their pictures; one woman even sent me a photo of her naked on her Harley. As a policeman, I'm not used to this.

"Everyone asks about my hair. Shaving it off was the best thing I've ever done. It was blond and thinning anyway, and I always kept it really short after my years in the Marine Corps. It was executive producer Richard Dominick's idea for me to shave it completely. I was pretty nervous about it, but he thought it would make me more recognizable. So I took a razor to it. Immediately, there was a huge reaction from everybody—the staff, the audience, the guests (female strippers constantly ask to buff my head with their butts!). I love the bald look. It's not only that I'm more recognizable, it's so easy to maintain. I use a regular razor and shaving cream. Now it takes about ten minutes because I know how to do it. That first time I botched it up so bad it looked like I had been in a car accident. But I don't shave every day because it's like shaving a whale; it's just too big. Another good thing is that both on the police force and on the show, I don't have to worry anymore about anybody grabbing my hair!

"Actually, breaking up fights on the show is usually pretty easy. I'm a nice guy and I get along with everybody, but I'm tough when I have to be. When people start acting goofy and get out of line, then my demeanor changes. I can kick ass just like everybody else does.

"Somewhere along the way in working these shows I developed the strategy of coming up behind people and grabbing their clothes. You never want to step between people because then you take the impact. Grabbing their clothes is really safer for the guests, too.

ARE YOU PREGNANT RIGHT NOW BY A MAN WHO'S MARRIED OR DATING SOMEONE ELSE?

"But we have plenty of guys onstage to handle anything. Only once was it really tough; when two guys on the show were all-state wrestlers. They were fast and strong and they knew how to get out of our holds. They were throwing us, and the fight kept going on and on. The Klan shows are also interesting because the audience gets so riled up. Dealing with transsexuals is also a challenge. In the show 'I'm Pregnant by a Transsexual,' Brittany, who is really a man, was pushing me and screaming at me. After that show aired I went to my police job and everyone was taunting, 'That woman was kicking your ass!' But that was no woman. That was a big dude.

"People think I'm cool now, but that's because they didn't know me in junior high school. Back then I was this skinny little runt, maybe 135 pounds, with a nerdy haircut and glasses. But I started lifting weights in high school, I let my hair grow long, and got contact lenses. My neck probably doubled in size, and my weight shot up to about 245 pounds. I show people pictures from before and they can't stop laughing. It's quite a change from the tough-guy glossy we send out now to my fans! "

Todd Schultz

"This show is great because everyone is here to have fun; that's what it's all about, for our guests, the audience, even the staff.

"Like Steve, when I applied to the show in 1994—a few months after Steve came on—I had no clue who this guy Jerry Springer was. I was working as a production assistant in films and all of a sudden the business here in Chicago picked up and moved to L.A. So my friend suggested I try the talk shows in this area. I applied to *Oprah*, *Jenny*, and *Jerry*, and got a call back from *Jerry* right away and I was soon hired.

"One of my favorite parts of the job is hanging out with Jerry. And I also love that it's different every day. The shows may seem the same—the fighting, the cheating—but really you see and hear new things all the time. My wildest story will always be the time we had some transsexuals on the show. I'm looking for the 'gaffer tape' we use to hang lights and such and someone tells me the guests have it in the green room. I can't imagine what they would need it for but I go in there and hear all this tape ripping. The transsexuals are using it to tape their thingies between their legs! I ran out of there so fast I don't think Carl Lewis could have beaten me that day.

"I started helping with security pretty soon after I was hired. Steve didn't have much of a budget back then, so when he would be working a show he would say, 'Todd's a big guy. Let's get him here to help me.' (I'm the only show security guy who has no police experience.) It reminds me of when I was a little kid and I'd go wrestle with my brother. I've been bruised and scratched, but luckily that's about it.

"My best fight was the first nude one we ever had. This stripper was giving a lap dance to a woman's fiancé, and the minute the stripper straddled the guy's legs the woman gets up and grabs for the stripper's hair. They start wrestling on the floor. Steve gets the girl with the clothes on but another security guy and I grab the stripper around the waist. We pick her up and suddenly realize, 'Oh my God. We're touching a naked chick!,' and we drop her. We weren't touching anywhere we weren't supposed to, we were just startled. So she gets up and charges after the other woman, and we're

ARE YOU MARRIED TO OR DATING A MAN WHO HAS ANOTHER WOMAN PREGNANT WITH HIS CHILD RIGHT NOW?

trying to stop her wondering where we are going to grab. Finally we got hold of her arm and broke the fight up.

"I do help stop the fights quite a bit, but mostly I'm becoming known for my role as the 'show dork.' When something dumb or funny has to be done, I get called out to do it. One time a 300-pound, 60-year-old grandmother came on who was still stripping. She called me on stage and gave me a little lap dance. Another time a transsexual announced she had a crush on me, and the producers made me go out and sit next to her!

"How did I get this role? In one show a few of the girls suddenly announced that they had a crush on me. Two girls danced with me onstage and one gave me a backrub. I'm lying there getting this backrub, acting like I'm swimming in the sea, and Jerry cracks, 'You know, the good thing about this, Todd, is you're contributing to saving the whales,' remarking on how big I was. Then Jerry started making comments about me on other occasions, like saying the headset I wear isn't plugged into anything, that I just talk to the air. I'd play up to it, have a good time. But Jerry would feel bad and give me Bulls tickets. We're talking sixth row, right behind Mike! So I started telling him, 'Make fun of me as much as you want!'

"Being on TV has made me more conscious of my appearance. I mean you can't go out there looking like a slob. When my grandmother called me and said she saw me on TV, she asked, 'What's that sticking out underneath your arms?' I took the hint: I'm motivated now! Especially since executive producer Richard Dominick has been letting Steve and me do some shows with Jerry. We did *Leno* and *Letterman, Talk Soup*. We even did a sitcom, *Between Brothers*, on UPN. It was great. Instead of looking like mean thugs, like we do on other shows, they gave us some lines."

Showtime!

I t's fifteen minutes before showtime and the offices inside the *Jerry Springer Show* are surprisingly tranquil. Jerry still sits in his office, in casual clothes—having not yet been briefed on the day's guests. Producers, stage hands, and other staffers mill around quietly, pulling together loose ends. But the calm is deceptive, for in just a few minutes one of the wildest shows on television will explode with all the power and passion of a professional wrestling match.

Most people are surprised to learn that Jerry knows almost as little about the guests' situations as the viewers do. But he has always preferred it this way. Right before showtime, Jerry gets a two-minute briefing on the day's players. Even then he learns only about the guests for the first segment. He will be briefed about subsequent segments during each commercial break. By not knowing the particulars, Jerry can react spontaneously, with the same surprise and emotion as the viewers at home. As Jerry dons his trademark Armani suit, stage manager Todd Schultz is out on stage, getting the studio audience pumped.

Hey, This Isn't a Comedy Club

Todd's job is to lay down the basic rules: "No. 1, have a great time!" He cautions the audience that they are not allowed to promote fighting among the guests. And, since the show purposely lacks a light-up APPLAUSE sign, he asks the audience to watch him on occasion, reacting to events when he gives the signal. "I don't tell them what to do because I want an honest reaction," Todd says. The producers want clean language from the audience as much as from the guests; spectators are asked to limit themselves to "oooh," "aaah," "boo," or the ever-expressive "Jerry! Jerry!" (plus applause, of course). As Todd wraps up his act, Jerry emerges to cheers and addresses the crowd. He proceeds to tell the exact same jokes that he has since the very first show.

"A guy was caught with his hand in my pocket. I asked him what he was doing and he said, 'Looking for change.' I said, 'Why didn't you just ask me?' and he said, 'I don't talk to strangers.' "

"I was in L.A. and this gorgeous woman was pounding on my hotel room door for two hours.... So finally I let her out."

"Funerals for these jokes will be held tomorrow morning."

Lights, Camera, and Plenty of Action

When Steve comes on to take his place in the "hot seat" the crowd bursts into spontaneous cheers—they know that the warm-up is over and the title bout is ready to begin. Richard Dominick commandeers the show from his podium just off

23

to the side of the stage; senior producer Rachelle Consiglio stands at his side with her own monitor, and next to her is the producer of that particular show, standing by for on-the-fly instructions on how to improve the show (changes are often made on the floor to heighten the intensity). Andrew Savage also stands by to give immediate judgments and advice.

When Jerry dashes back onto the floor and the red light on the camera goes on, the small studio rocks with thunderous applause, a palpable sense of anticipation, and cries of "Jerry! Jerry!" And there is Jerry, with that familiar little blue card in hand, ready to launch us on an adventure to who knows where. In fact, the cards provide no more than a brief Who's Who for the episode, with the names and core descriptions (e.g., "Heather, pregnant with boyfriend's baby; Dave, boyfriend who is seeing another man on the side..."). No questions are prewritten, no one-liners preplanned.

As is obvious to anyone who watches the show, guests are not pre-scripted either. The choice words they use, the actions they perform—be it getting down on one knee to propose or battling it out with their two-timing husband—are totally left to their discretion. "Mostly, we tell the guests just to energetically convey their story, not to wait for Jerry to pull it out of them," says Consiglio.

Guests do reveal to the producers during the earlier screening process their approximate game-plan. But they can't know for sure how they will respond to a situation until they are smack in the middle of it. For example, one woman guessed that she would not react much to her partner's admission that he was cheating on her, since he had showed up in the hospital the day after she went into labor with their child—his neck plastered with hickies! Yet when he brought the other woman onstage, the woman bawled her eyes out.

That spontaneity can be great—as when a man who planned to leave his girlfriend suddenly proposed to her instead, or when a guy pulled his girlfriend's panties from his shirt pocket and admitted he sniffs them throughout the day. Then there was the episode that was originally planned as a sedate human interest piece on a woman born without arms or legs. But when her boyfriend joined her onstage, he was rude and distant, eventually admitting he was no longer in love with her. The woman's parents stormed out screaming, especially after he decided to dump her on the show.

Meanwhile, Inside the Control Room

Watching the zaniness of the *Jerry Springer Show* live is an enthralling experience, kind of like seeing a Chicago Bulls game, wrestling match, and soap opera all in one. The task of transferring that heightened energy to viewers at home falls to the show's longtime director, Greg Klazura. Greg's job is somewhat akin to directing a sporting event—but tougher. "In sports, at least you know that if the football is on the 25 yard line, they're going to advance. We never know what's going to happen, so sometimes we go in the wrong direction!" he says.

While the fights may be dramatic and obvious, much of the excitement is actually small, swift, and easily overlooked. "If someone pulls out a dildo and our camera misses it, the people at home have no idea what happened,"

ARE YOU IN LOVE WITH SOMEONE WHO HAS ANOTHER LOVER AND YOU WANT THEM TO MAKE A CHOICE ONCE AND FOR ALL?

Greg says. The same holds true when someone hurls a condom or their wedding ring. Greg even has to be sure the cameras don't miss action in the audience, such as the time a woman asking a question was insulted by an onstage guest, and responded by flashing her breasts and crotch.

Of course, in a show like this one, where producers aim to bring in episodes that can be watched with the sound off, there is an incredible amount of action, and action is a director's dream. Take the infamous episode, "I Married a Horse." The man could go on for hours about his love affair with his horse, but the message landed like a bullet in the one second the camera caught the pair French kissing. "The whole idea for television is that you want to make it as graphic as possible, and only a guy who really loves his horse is going to put his tongue into her mouth. For a director on a show, that's the greatest thing that could happen," says Greg.

A Final Thought on Those Final Thoughts

Finally, it's time for Jerry's "Final Thought," that moment when Jerry gives us the moral of the story. He writes these summations the morning before the show, based on what he knows is the episode's general theme.

Why does he do it? Even Jerry is not sure. "It wasn't part of any grand strategy," he observes. He had been doing commentaries on serious news topics during his TV anchorman days, and when he started the talk show its aim was to be an earnest program as well. The company that owned his show also owned the *Donahue* show, and since Phil was retiring there was talk of making Jerry as philosophical— and as successful—as Phil. It seemed natural for Jerry to continue the commentaries for which he was already known. As the show veered from the headlines to the crotchlines, the serious-toned commentaries incongruously continued.

To Jerry, the ridiculousness of his serious summations following the likes of these shows has actually increased their attraction. "I think that, very subtly, there's a sort of comedy in it because you've seen all this craziness, and now all of a sudden I'm giving like a State of the Union address."

Thanks for Coming

Viewing a *Jerry Springer Show* live is the ultimate experience. Getting riled up by all those battles, chanting "Jerry! Jerry! Jerry!" with the rest of the crowd, seeing all that raw emotion up close and uncensored. Before setting the enlivened crowd back on the street, Jerry and security chief Steve Wilkos personally greet all 250 audience members—a process that usually takes about half an hour. And in the background, you'll occasionally hear a solicitation for future panel members (as Todd calls out, "If you want to confront the Klan next Tuesday, come see me). Everything goes according to schedule, smooth as can be—except for the action during the taping.

JERRY *Springer*

ARE YOU TORN BETWEEN TWO LOVERS AND WANT TO END IT WITH ONE OF THEM?

"I don't know
call this a talk
anybody does

Holiday Hell with My Feuding Family

Donna and hubby: today's main course.

Donna dishes it out.

Richard serves it up.

ou'll never be able to complain about holidays with your own family again. This clan says its constant fighting has made it hard even to congregate for Christmas, so everyone has agreed to break bread on the neutral ground of the show. But no more than five minutes into the program, the food fights start. At the center of it all are Donna and Richard, who have been on the show before, since Richard had affairs with both her aunt and her cousin. But once you get a taste of Donna—the firestorm at the center of a wild family—you start to understand why. Unrepentant Richard is a big part of the problem, but it appears this family fell apart long before he came on the scene.

Aired December 23, 1994

She's got a bone to pick with her mother.

Notable Numbers

2 (number of children Richard and Donna have together)

2 (number of Donna's relatives Richard has boinked)

2 (number of seemingly normal relatives of the 10 onstage)

The Mother Who Loves Too Little

As the show opens, it looks like this family might actually have a nice meal. The table is set with china and crystal. Turkey and all the trimmings are in view. Donna, her husband Richard, and her petite mother Brenda wear their holiday finery.

But revelations quickly belie this placid family scene. Richard and Donna have separated due to Richard's infidelity with her cousin and aunt: **"I hate his guts,"** Donna declares.

She is full of anger for her entire family, not just Richard. **"I don't want to spend no holidays with none of them no more."** As for her mother: **"I'm tired of her telling me 'If you never married him, you wouldn't have gotten hurt.'"** Even if her mother was right about Richard. **"You was right. National TV knows you was right. So drop it. Move on."**

But Brenda feels Donna has always ignored her advice. **"You don't listen. I told you to lose weight, too, but you still don't listen."** Suddenly, Donna grabs the turkey and smacks her mother with it. Richard hurls a bowl of sweet potato pie on Donna. Before security can stop the food fight, Donna is wearing white melted marshmallow all over her dress and hair.

The Embarrassed Aunties

We meet two of Brenda's sisters, Joyce and Karen. They say that these antics aren't hyped up for the cameras. Joyce blames Brenda, because she's determined to control Donna's every thought and movement.

Jerry can't believe this family's behavior. Jerry: **I am asked this question all the time, "Where do you find the people to come on**

"If you don't want to lose weight, then eat the turkey, don't throw it on her!"

these shows?" And I am compelled to ask you.

Brenda: **Well, this family's unreal anyway.**

Jerry: **But you're the head of the family, and you are sitting next to a daughter who has sweet potato on her head.**

The Aunt Who Loved Too Much

The adulterous Aunt Dodi feels little remorse for sleeping with her niece's husband and blames the family's problems on jealousy among the sisters and mother. **"Donna gets jealous because of the relationship her mom has with the sisters."**

She responds: **Yeah (sadly), I do. Now that me and Richard are separated I don't have nobody. You see what all my aunts are like. They're all ho's.**

Aunt Karen: **You can turn to me and come to my house, but don't throw food on it.**

Donna: **Did I throw food at you? Do you want me to throw food at you?**

Jerry (jumping up to stage): **No! No! Please, do not throw food. This is a rented suit!**

Eventually, Dodi comes close to an apology. **"I would just like to see once and for all some peace."** Donna proposes a toast—which she then launches into Dodi's lap.

Isn't this family embarrassed by their behavior? Jerry asks, **"What happens when you go back to your neighborhood and they see the show?"**

"I dye my hair for the first week," notes Karen.

Though he remains largely silent, Richard, of course, is

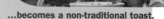

A traditional toast...

...becomes a non-traditional toast.

Cousin Shawn: "Just because I slept with one guy you know does not make me a whore."

Humble pie it isn't.

hardly the innocent one. He is sorry he got caught sleeping with Donna's relatives, he says, but seems more remorseful for the discovery than for the deed.

The Other, Other Woman

Cousin Shawn, who also had an affair with Richard, joins the table. Like everyone else in this gang, Shawn isn't apologetic.
Shawn: **Our family does not revolve around Donna and Richard, and that's why Donna is such a bitch, because she wants it to.**
Donna: **I might be a bitch, but I'm not a [bleep]ing whore.**

Shawn says she is no longer sleeping with Richard. **"Now that Donna knows, it's no fun because there's no risk."**

When someone implies that Richard's sexual appetite is unstoppable, he jumps to correct the record:
Richard: **I haven't slept with all of the aunts.**
Jerry: **Just because you haven't slept with every one of them, you don't get a reward.**
Donna: **Here is your reward!**

Donna smashes Richard with more turkey. In response, Richard gives Donna a big kiss—then tosses pie all over her face. **"What was worse,"** Jerry quips, **"the kiss or the whipped cream?"**

Feeling the Pain

When an audience member criticizes Donna for not treating others with the respect she herself so craves, Donna lashes out at her. **"You go through the hell I went through and**

let your boyfriend screw everybody else and then you get up here and see how you can react. Until then, sit your ass down!"

Donna may be reacting like an angry woman, but she is deeply pained inside. Jerry puts his finger on the family's curse when he tells Brenda, **"When your children were young, you didn't tell them enough that, no matter what they felt inside, that they were loved. And so now everybody's a bitch, everybody's a ho."** Tears well in Donna's eyes as she softly admits, **"I am hurt. Especially when my mother gets on national TV and says I'm fat."** She breaks down completely when an audience member shouts, **"You're beautiful, Donna."**

What's It All About, Jerry?

"They say that blood is thicker than water. Not so in this family. Here the blood seems so thin we can't stop the bleeding. The holiday invites them to come together again, but they need to share concern before they share a meal. Simply continuing this malicious treatment of each other suggests that the real turkey is not necessarily on the table, but around it.

"Till next time, take care of yourself and each other."

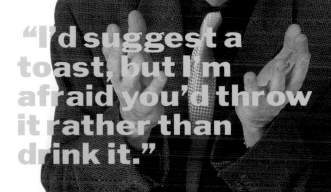

"I'd suggest a toast, but I'm afraid you'd throw it rather than drink it."

My Wife Is A Dominatrix

Some people enjoy playing master/slave games in the bedroom, but for others, S&M is a way of life. And for others still, it's not just a hobby—it's a job. In this episode we meet leather-clad men and women of all types: your basic dominant and slave, a disturbing youngster and his outraged parents, and even a man who is pissed off that his wife the professional dominatrix has stopped charging a favored client (and now she has him cooking for her and kissing her feet for free!). All that plus homemade footage of a dominatrix at the "office."

Aired January 4, 1995

The Couple

He wears one leather glove and carries a whip—but he's neither Michael Jackson nor Indiana Jones. No, Wolfie is a longtime practitioner of S&M and his wife Sabrina, is now his personal slave. In the vernacular, Wolfie is a **"dominant,"** the proper term for the male equivalent of a **"dominatrix."**

As he tells it, the vassal role is good for Sabrina and her self-image: **"My wife knew she had a very submissive side to her. She enjoyed someone who was a much more powerful person."**

"You're telling me having a wife as a slave helps her self-esteem?" asks Jerry.

Being submissive means that Sabrina spends all of her non-work time serving her husband. She bathes him, prepares his food, and is completely subservient. **"She is naked at all times in my presence when we are alone in our apartment."** On weekend evenings, Sabrina is constantly chained to the bed. Wolfie walks backstage and leads out his wife by a leash

"How does a whip help her with her weight? What do you do, beat it off of her?"

Wolfie says, "I help her bring up her self-esteem."

Bart says, "I'm learning to live life how I'd like to."

Mom says, "This kid needs to get his ass back in college."

Jerry says, "Bad dog! Bad dog!"

attached to a silver choker around her neck. Her hands are tied behind her back, her mouth gagged with a leather strap.

"**Assume the position,**" he commands, and she obediently kneels at his feet. Her gag is removed.

Jerry: **Look at you. You're a human being. Why are you doing that?**

Sabrina: **I enjoy it.**

Jerry: **Wouldn't you want to be in a relationship on equal terms?**

Sabrina: **I consider that it is equal terms. It's just that we've got a different kind of relationship. I have always been attracted to men who are stronger.**

Jerry: **If the only way he's stronger is by having you chained up, then he's not stronger.** (The audience cheers.)

Jerry begs Sabrina to take the empty seat near her husband, but she demurs: **"No, I'm fine, thank you."** He asks Wolfie whether he ever hits her. **"That's a loaded question. Do I hit her in anger? No."**

"You hit her for fun?" Jerry queries.

"Spanking, yes. But I never hit her in the face or anything."

The Businesswoman

Ava has made humiliating men her life's profession. And that was fine with her husband Mark until Ava stopped charging her favorite client, Bart. Now Mark thinks the two might be having an affair, a notion Ava dismisses as childish and ridiculous.

For one thing, there's nothing sexual about their encounters, according to Ava: **"There's no genital contact, no breast contact. When he comes over, basically, he cleans the house and cooks meals. And also to worship my feet, to rub my feet. Every woman should own one. It's wonderful."** (Jerry promises that later, we'll see a video documenting what really goes on between the pair.)

Impeccably dressed in a suit and tie, Bart joins the panel. He kisses Ava's hand and he, too, kneels at her feet. Ava assures Jerry that this is a **"sign of respect,"** and that Bart **"enjoys this."** Bart agrees: **"I screwed up my life enough on my own. I needed someone to teach me how to live."** Hubby Mark, however, is not amused. He leers at Bart. **"Why don't you sit down like a normal person."** But, as Ava points out, **"you don't complain much when he cooks dinner."**

Notable Numbers

• 8–10% (American households that own some dominance or bondage gear)

• 11% (women who have experienced S&M, according to a study)

• 14% (men who have)

Damien, Beverly and Brian's baby boy.

Damien, with his new "family" and his parents.

"Who wouldn't worship me?"

Her roommates, for starters.

The Appalled Parents—and Their Troubled Son

Beverly and Brian are mortified that their son Damien is into this lifestyle. Damien quit college to get involved with an outrageous band. Beverly cries: **"They go onstage, they put him on racks. They torture him, throw blood on him, put him in cages. It's like Alice Cooper gone crazy."** As if that's not enough, Damien has also taken to piercing sensitive body parts onstage. **"This kid needs to get his ass back home in college."**

But as we see, though she pursues a **"normal"** lifestyle, Damien's mother is two steps away from a riding crop herself. As Jerry diplomatically puts it, there's an **"aggressiveness in your style."**

As Damien enters sporting a "shirt" of studded black leather straps crisscrossing his chest, he casually says, **"Hi, Ma."** The audience chants, **"Freak! Freak! Freak!"** Having left home, Damien lives with dominatrix Valkyrie (a computer consultant by day) and together they dominate his girlfriend Raven (she, too, enters on a leash and sits at his feet). Apparently there's a hierarchy to S&M. **"You start from the bottom and go to the top,"** Damien reports.

Raven: **I can't be a master yet. I have a lot to learn.**
Jerry: **How hard can it be? You just boss people around.**
Damien: **No. There's certain places on the body where you do not whip. And you have to learn what textures do which....**
Beverly: **And this coming from a kid who gets his balls pierced onstage!** [As well as, we later discover, his nipples, tongue, and penis.] **This kid was an alter boy. He went to Catholic school for nine years!**
Damien: **And look what the Catholic Church did to me, Mom!**

Damien says at home he's **"more mentally and physically abused by my parents than I ever am in the S&M scene."** Looking at the domineering Beverly you suspect he has a point. As Valkyrie aptly puts it, **"How can his mom be so against something**

Jeers

When Wolfie's wife deferentially sits down at her master's feet.

Cheers

When Ava's slave Bart performs the same actions (thanks to the double standard held by the mostly female crowd).

she herself is so good at? She wants to control every single aspect of his life."

Beverly responds: **"No. I want this boy back in school and away from freaks like you!"** Suddenly Bart gets up to shout at her, but he's quickly ordered, **"On your knees! On your knees!"** Valkyrie and Damien temporarily leave the stage.

"Take that smile off your face now."

The Roommate from Hell

Keith and Mandy live with Daphne, another professional dominatrix who gets paid to order men to **"fold her underwear, do her nails, and change her oil."** Being as overweight and overbearing as a prison warden apparently hasn't affected Daphne's sense of self-esteem. **"Look at me. I'm beautiful."**

Let's Go to the Videotape

In the educational portion of our show, Valkyrie steps up to defend S&M's much-maligned reputation. First of all, everyone is a willing participant who can leave at any time, she informs us. **"It isn't just spanking, whipping, and wearing leather."** Being a slave **"is about respecting a person so much and trusting them so much you let them do what they will with you,"** and being a master means **"taking responsibility for someone; caring totally and completely for someone."**

But spanking, whipping, and wearing leather are at least the means to that end. Jerry shows the long-promised black-and-white video of Ava and Bart. (No wonder Mark is miffed; with all the torture apparatus around, there's no comfortable place to sit in his living room!) She blindfolds Bart, then cracks the whip on his butt:

Ava: **In a few minutes, it's going to sting so badly you're not going to want to sit on it for quite a while. Do you understand me?**

Bart: **Yes, mistress.**

Ava (whipping him again): **Look straight ahead, and take that smile off your face—now!**

What's It All About, Jerry?

"Some apparently get a sexual kick out of engaging in such master/slave role-playing. But even if consenting adults think this is okay in the bedroom as a game, it can't be healthy if it becomes a lifestyle. The danger is that whatever entices one to such behavior may reappear in that person's other relationships with people who aren't into these games, and the consequences could be terribly destructive. If this starts to be a way of life and not just a momentary fantasy, you might ask yourself, 'Why is this a turn-on?' If you need to get hurt, maybe you already are. It's time to get help.

"Till next time, take care of yourself and each other."

All I Need to Know I Learned from *Springer:*

• Men actually pay for the privilege of cooking and cleaning for a woman, and enjoy being put on a leash and ordered around.

• A male dominatrix is called a dominant.

• Being a master is not about whipping other people, all appearances to the contrary.

• If you want to get into S&M, you'll need lots of black clothes, with lots of holes in them.

I Slept with 251 Men in 10 Hours!

*J*ust as the show title proclaims, Annabel Chong had sex with 251 men in just 10 hours. This apparently gives her claim to the world's sex record, beating the previous mark of 120 by a wide open margin, so to speak. But it wasn't all just fun; Annabel is a porn queen, and the stunt was recorded and released on a four-hour videotape, bringing her fame and fortune. In her exclusive interview on *Springer*, Annabel bares all about what made her do it, and is confronted by a few of her supporting actors and their less-than-supporting wives.

Aired May 1, 1995

She took on all comers.

The champ enters the ring.

She's on Top

The Queen is introduced—to a chorus of astonishment from the women in the audience. The facts of the matter are pretty straight-forward; the motivation and morals are more complex. Jerry gets right to the heart of things when he asks, **"Why?"**

Annabel's simple answer: **"It's never been done before."** To her, **"it's no different from having sex for 10 hours with one guy, and I've done that before."**

Jerry points out that some people feel this is immoral, sick, and dangerous. He wonders how she even conceived of this idea. Annabel explains that her porn-producer boss suggested **"the world's biggest gang bang"** at lunch one day. Annabel decided the idea was superb: **"I kind of figured it out. I hate going on dates, but I still want to get laid. So that is 251 less dates to do."**

She admits the experience was a bit uncomfortable—but mostly from guys digging their nails into her. Jerry tries to figure out how much time each guy was allotted—with groups of five, it would seem they were rotated every 10 minutes. But things were not that rigid, so to speak: **"If you were going strong, it was like, longer."**

And where did the men come from? Invitations for participants were made in porn magazines and videos. Contenders sent in an application form, plus a photo of themselves. "A lot of guys sent Polaroids of their penises. Usually if a guy sent a nude photo of himself, he got in." Annabel selected the first 100, but, weary of the hard work, let her producer choose the rest.

The XXX Movie

Jerry plays some of the few portions of the porn video made from the event that can be aired on TV. We see the producer telling the guys they're going to try to reach 300, so anyone who wants to go around more than once can do so. A sweaty Annabel is seen on her back, as groups of naked guys approach her lair. One man has a pragmatic question: Which way to lie? A makeshift scoreboard tracks Annabel's progress.

Bad Boys

Mick and Richard, two of Annabel's conquests, now join her onstage. But Mick has a wife of 11 years and Richard a longstanding steady girlfriend of his own. Mick describes how he came to participate:

Mick: **I took a video home and we were watching it. It was a Christmas video with a bunch of Santa Clauses. And at the end of the video Annabel was asking for people to help with her event.**

Jerry: **You were in the Christmas spirit of giving, by gosh.**

Mick: **My wife says, "I dare you." It was an attack on my male ego and a dare, so I mailed it in not thinking that I'd have a chance in hell.**

Jerry: **You may now go to hell!**

Mick is sorry that his wife has now turned on him, particuarly since it was her prompting that egged him on. Mick admits he enjoyed himself, even though the encounter wasn't romantic. He jokes: **"I would rather have spent a week in the Bahamas with Annabel, but it just didn't happen that way."**

To Richard, this was **"the opportunity of a lifetime."** But his girlfriend Stephanie is furious: **"It's the macho, 'I got to impress my male friends.' Well you go ahead and do that because now you're going to be alone."** Richard is unrepentant; he tells Jerry that **"this is the year of the pig, and I just feel that I started the year off right."**

Jerry underscores the experience by showing the women portions of the video that involve their men—segments deemed too hot to show on TV, or even to the studio audience because, says Jerry, **"then we are no better than the people who make the video."** Both women are mortified.

Jerry displays the evidence.

And reveals his own naughty side.

Update: Picking Up the Gauntlet

Though Annabel's record seems astonishing, it did not stand for long. Another porn star, and previous *Springer* guest, Jasmin St. Clair teamed up with the same producer and had sex with 300 men in 10 hours, again documenting the whole procedure on videotape. And she shares her tale in another exclusive *Springer* appearance. Unlike Annabel, though, Jasmin does admit to experiencing some discomfort: "I was being packed with ice in the middle of the event. I was in extreme pain." On the same show, we meet another fluff girl, Candy Apples, and Sterling, a self-described nympho-maniac, both of whom declare their intentions to try and break the record again. Stay tuned.

Two of the 251 were Richard (right) and Mick,

But to his wife…

…And his girlfriend, they're just known as "Dick."

The Fluff Girl

Lest you think a woman can service 251 men all by herself, we are introduced to Sinnamon, a **"fluff girl"**—apparently a common term in her industry. Sinnamon's sister, Toi, offers a definition: **"A fluff girl is somebody that [bleeps] every guy before they do Annabel."** In her own words, Sinnamon was directed to **"do whatever it took to get the guys excited."** Whatever apparently included staging a **"girl-girl"** show where three of the women involved themselves with each other. She's ready to spill more details, but Jerry has heard quite enough, thank you.

Before everyone gets too caught up in guilt and blame, sex-crazed Annabel offers up a high-minded philosophical perspective: **"It's a pity that in our very Judeo-Christian society something like this causes a lot of problems. Last time in Babylon, they had the temple of the goddess Astarte, and they had priestess-prostitutes having sex with men as a celebration of fertility and life."**

Jerry reminds her that she wasn't celebrating anything; she was making a porn video. Annabel corrects him: **"Lying down to get screwed is a wonderful experience. I feel alive."**

Jerry's Confession

A chagrined Jerry has a confession of his own. **"My slate isn't that clean either. I should tell you now what I did last night."** A humorous video shows him in silk pajamas, surrounded by three breathtaking beauties in skimpy teddies. As Jerry pours champagne, each offers an evaluation: Jerry was **"great,"** **"amazing,"** and unlike any other man.

Back in the studio, Jerry quickly corrects the record. **"I was just dreaming that. This is what really happened to me last night."** He shows another tape, featuring a lonely Jerry wearing a ratty robe and watching *Gilligan's Island* while downing a vat of ice cream.

Unrepentant, Unforgiven

Participant number 20, Matt, joins the panel, along with his ex-girlfriend Beth. This charming fellow participated in the orgy and then came home that night and had sex with Beth, without telling her what he did. **"I think you are a lying, egotistical bastard."** He responds, **"I was just trying to celebrate my freedom just like everybody else."**

What Would You Do if That Was Your Man?

Jerry asked some women on the street:

• "It would be a good thing his insurance is paid up."

• "I'd 'Lorena Bobbitt' him!"

• "He'd come home to find all his stuff out in front of the door. The credit cards would be canceled, the locks would be changed. He'd be gone, gone, gone."

Here is the "fluff girl" Sinnamon on stage.

Here is the "fluff girl" at work.

Last Man Standing

For a closing treat we meet porn star Ron Jeremy, who produced the final climax by being No. 251. He is given a boisterous welcome from many audience members, some of whom must recognize him from his oeuvre of 1,000 movies.

Audience members get the final words in, including one man who tells the men they are dogs and that **"I'm quite sure you're going to meet your maker one day."**

What's It All About, Jerry?

"This wasn't sex and it certainly wasn't lovemaking. No, this was nothing more than what I would consider consensual violence—violence to the body as well as to the notion of what is a woman. And despite what was said here today, I can't believe that the moment before they meet their maker, any of the 251 guys or the one woman will say of this record that this was their finest hour.

"Till next time, take care of yourself and each other."

All I Need to Know I Learned from Springer:

• Having sex with 251 guys hurts—but it's mostly from their digging nails.

• Modesty isn't helpful: Sending in a shot of your equipment will ensure you'll be chosen for one of these events.

• Never dare your man to participate in a gang bang.

• A fluff girl is like a supporting actress. If she does her job well, maybe she'll get a starring role herself someday.

"What was it like for you guys to sit there among a cattle of 251 others saying, 'Hey, I'm next?' Mooooo!"

My Pimp Is Ruining My Life!

Gina is a Chicago streetwalker who wants to leave her pimp. Not that she's found God or wants to change her lifestyle. She just wants to trade up to being a higher-class escort. But she is afraid to tell her pimp, Chi-Town so she has chosen to confront him in the safety of the *Springer Show.* As Jerry puts it, "we're getting an education here" in how things work on the streets. And what an education it is: We encounter a classically loquacious pimp, his all-business wife, a few of his other workers, and more.

Aired May 9, 1995

A Hooker's Lament:

"Over here is the place where a lot of the pimps and the girls go to drink coffee, warm up, run from the police. It's really sad. I never dreamed I would be doing this. Sometimes I sit out here, I think of my family, my mother, sisters, how I ended up here. I want so much for myself and it seems like I just will fall into these traps like this. I keep telling myself, you know, if I just hang out a little longer, things will get better."

"I swear, it's been in all the papers. Slavery's over."

The Unhappy Hooker

Gina wants her freedom.

Chi-Town, her pimp, declares, "I own her."

Gina's sisters are shocked to learn what she does.

These "sisters" are shocking to look at—but they stand up for Gina's rights.

Gina begins by telling Jerry how a nice girl like her got into a business like this. She was new to Chicago when she met a street tough who calls himself Chi-Town. The two began dating. **"He seemed like a really, really nice guy. We would go out and just kick it. We partied together and spent time together."**

Then one night Chi-Town unexpectedly told her to get out of the car and go pick up a john to demonstrate her devotion. Did she run? Did she hide? No, she got into a horny stranger's car, although she claims she was scared, angry—and fumbling. **"I told the guy, 'I have no idea what I'm doing. Just please be patient, bear with me.' Luckily he was a real nice guy."**

Jerry presses for more details, telling the audience, **"We're getting an education of what goes out on the streets."** Gina charged the man $40—for an unspecified act performed in his car—and then gave the money to Chi-Town. This one-time declaration of love quickly became a way of life. In exchange, Chi-Town provided an occasional place to live and other Sugar Daddy services. As Jerry puts it, **"You're a slave to this guy."**

Now, a year later, Gina finally wants to do what she should have done that first time: run, from the dangers of the streets and the mastery of her pimp. She still wants to be a hooker; she merely wishes to do it from the comforts of her own home. But Gina is scared to tell Chi-Town that she wants to leave him. **"You hear all kinds of stories about how pimps react to it when girls leave. You hear about them getting beat up, thrown out of the car, shot."**

He's a Master

Chi-Town admits he does **"own"** Gina, but says that in a way they own each other. **"I do whatever makes her happy, that's my job to do. Just like it's her job to make me happy."** In his eyes, he **"fulfills her every need."** And he has great admiration for her talent: **"Everybody can't play this game. She's one of the best that does this here."** When Jerry asks if Gina can leave, he says: **"It's mathematical impossible, Jerry."**

Gina touchingly tells Chi-Town that she did enter this profession of her own choosing, but is now ready to give it up. Gina: **I just want to leave peacefully.**
Chi-Town: **You know, statistics has proven once they leave, they have bad luck.**
Jerry: **What kind of bad luck is she going to run into? Will she not do well in the stock market?**
Chi-Town: **At this-here point in time, I can't have you to leave.**

Jerry presses Chi-Town to elaborate on what might happen. **"I don't mean I'm going to do anything physically."** Jerry sternly warns, **"I've got to tell you, these cameras are on,** and they go all over the country. And every police department in America is going to be watching. And nothing—I promise you—nothing is going to happen to her. Nothing."

Then Chi-town clarifies himself: **"You know what I mean by this here. Once somebody leave me and affiliate theyselves with some type of personal john or trick or whatever you call it just don't work out…. Bad luck would just naturally come to you and happen."**

Home Is Calling

Until Gina's sisters heard her confession backstage, they had no idea what she did for a living. Lisa and Lynn declare, **"We want to get Gina back home where she belongs."** But Gina has no intention of leaving the city. Even if she did, Chi-Town says he'll pursue her. **"She could be in Iraq, Iran, East Pakistan. From Maine to Spain, I will travel."**

Tricks of the Trade

The day before the show, Gina took Jerry and his cameraman on a field trip to her work site.
Chi-Town: **Gina exposed too much game to you, Jerry. She gave you too much, man.**
Jerry: **Yeah. Well now she's giving it to the rest of the country because we taped this.**

Jerry rolls the tape, which begins with Gina pointing out the location of her first **"date,"** apparently an industry term for a trick. Gina points out the adult book store where she often stands outside, waiting for men. For their $40, most men see their action in a nearby alley, or in their cars. Occasionally, Gina gets to rest on her back in a hotel bed when a guy rents one for an hour. **"Rain, snow, whatever, we are out here. Some of my best nights were in the rain."** The video ends with a saddened Gina hoping for a better life. But Chi-Town is unimpressed. **"I must fess up that that's a very touching film there. But I'm a pimp, man, you know."**

Others in the Biz

Savanah and Jasmine are transsexual prostitutes. They appear in full-blown drag. Savanah asks Gina how badly she wants to leave the business. **"Bad,"** she replies. And how soon? **"Today."** Savanah gets up and trades seats with Gina, so now **"she"** is next to Chi-Town.
Savanah: **I don't see how you can call yourself a man when you are getting ahead by standing on the**

"Talk to the hand."

Or talk to the "man" of the house, Caprice.

As Amber does here.

shoulders of this woman who, in a moment of weakness, decided that this would be the best thing for her.

Chi-Town: **I'm all man. You need to date a wimp and pay a pimp. And party. Talk to the hand** (lifts up his palm to Savanah).

Savanah: **Honey, talking to that hand is what you're going to have to do on a nightly basis when Gina leaves.**

That's Mrs. Pimp to You

A woman in the audience stands up to address Gina. **"If you want to leave, leave. He ain't going to stop you."** It turns out she would know—Caprice has been working for Chi-Town for a decade and is his common-law wife. When Jerry asks why she, too, turns all her ill-gotten gains over to Chi-Town, his seemingly innocent comment nearly starts an brawl:

Caprice: **Sometimes you get a little bit sarcastic and I don't like...**

Jerry: **Me?**

Caprice: **Yeah, you.**

Jerry: **I'm sorry.**

Next we meet Amber, a former employee

of Chi-Town's. She is here to say that as a pimp, **"he makes a lot of promises and don't keep them."** Caprice, now seated on stage, screams that Amber expected too much from Chi-Town: **"Baby, let me tell you something. You got to crawl before you can walk. You not going to get it slam, blam."**

Bye, Bye, Gina

Jerry has asked security man Steve to escort Gina safely out of the building. Chi-Town is non-plussed. He says he has spotted two guys in the front row who seem to be fans and he plans to take them under his wing. **"I'm going to lay the pimpology down. I'm going to introduce them to this here."** Jerry ask the men if they truly want to become pimps. **"If that's where the money's at,"** one answers.

What's It All About, Jerry?

"Understand, these women are not merely prostitutes; they are slaves. These women have hit bottom. And these guys who tell you they offer protection, in fact, offer these women nothing but hopelessness and a dead end, feeding off the desperation of young girls not yet strong enough to tell them to go to hell. These street walkers must know that selling your body is never a moral or wise thing to do, but selling it for someone else is insanity.

"Till next time, take care of yourself and each other."

Christmas with the Klan

"I understand that this is a big country and even people like you are permitted in it."

In a completely new take of a "white" Christmas, the Ku Klux Klan display their holiday message of anger and hate. As Jerry warns, it's a show that is "difficult to watch." Taped footage takes us to a Klan Christmas party—where guests trade lynching nooses and swastika cookies—and a Klan baptism. The adult Klansmen are practically clownish ("This reaches the point of not being personally offensive because it's so stupid," says Jerry); the most poignant and disturbing revelations are when we see the young son of one Klan couple commanding his toy monkey to "Die! Die!" At the show's conclusion, the audience gets to turn the tables by handing the Klansmen clever holiday presents of their own.

Aired December 20, 1995

Here comes "Klanta Claus."

"Klanta's" real-life son, Michael.

The real tragedy is that this boy is being taught to hate.

Here Comes Klanta Claus

There may be no holiday more sacred in Christianity than Christmas, but the way these Klansmen celebrate it, Jesus would no doubt insist on canceling the whole affair. As Jerry points out, members of this group **"are taking this most sacred of holidays and perverting it and basically teaching their children exactly the opposite message."**

First onstage is "Klanta Claus," a man who could pass for Santa but for the swastika on his sleeve and the profanities spewing from his lips. **"I've got a bag of goodies for all these people here, especially the Niggers,"** he says. Jerry pounces: **"Here's the rule. You are entitled, as any other citizen, to be on this show. But you will not use that term here again."** Jerry also wants to set the record straight for any naïve children watching: **"This is not Santa Claus."**

Jerry is mortified that this man is teaching hatred to his young son. A camera shows the child and his mother backstage, wearing matching Klan robes and hoods. Jerry asks the young boy what Christmas means to him. **"Oh, I don't know,"** the boy responds. Then he shakes a toy with a monkey attached to a stick and cries out, **"Die! Die!"** His father is proud of this unconscionable behavior. **"My son used to go a white boys' school. Now all these blacks come in and he has picked up the black language. They've ruined their own neighborhoods, so now they come to the white boys' neighborhood and are ruining theirs."** Jerry charges the father with committing a form of **"child abuse"** by teaching the boy such zealous hatred.

King of the Klan

J.D. Alder, head of the Klan group The Invisible Empire, enters to the boos of the audience, wearing a blue Superman-like getup with a Klan insignia in place of the "S." **"Praise God for AIDS,"** he says, **"That would get rid of a lot of these porch monkeys."** Replies Jerry, **"You better hope God is forgiving."**

J.D. wants to make it look more like Christmas on the

The Bigotry Bakery

"No Klan Christmas party would be complete without these goodies":
- hooded Klansmen gingerbreads
- chocolate swastika sweets
- blood-red Jewish star cookies
- blood-drop cake

There are three of them, but they coming bearing strange gifts.

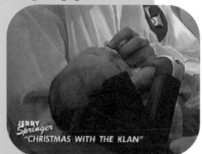

This baby is being baptized into the Klan.

The Klansmen unveil their tree.

Complete with ornaments.

stage. **"Nothing is going to make this look like Christmas,"** Jerry retorts. But J.D. is already up, unveiling a large tree with a swastika in place of the star.

Jerry rolls a tape of J.D. performing a baptism of sorts on a newborn: **"Ariana, as the newest member of our race, we bless you in the hopes that your life will be long, prosperous, and white-oriented. We dedicate you to the race destined to rule for all eternity."** Back in the studio, Jerry is beside himself with anger. **"J.D., what you have done to that child you will rot in hell for."**

Who Is That Masked Man?

Also on stage, covered by the trademark hood, is Vince, a young man who joined the Klan after he met them while they were protesting the removal of Klan merchandise from a flea market.

Jerry isn't about to let Vince hide his identity. He offers a deal: **"If you are willing to drop out of the Klan, I'll let you walk off this stage and no one will ever know that you were here, and you will be converted. But if you stay on, you'll show America who you are. You will pay the consequences of your beliefs."** After first trying to get away with removing the hood by hiding behind a rebel-flag scarf, Vince finally reveals his face. **"I take it back. Cover it up,"** Jerry responds.

Holiday at Home

Jerry shows another video, this time of a Christmas celebration at a Klansman's house in Florida. J.D. Alder offers his greeting: **"We are gathered here tonight to celebrate a white Christmas, a Christmas with multicolored lights instead of the damned Jew white product of light bushes that we've got in the department store."** One man receives a noose as a present: **"Just what I needed."**

The Night Before Damnation

A videotape is shown of a Klan leader reciting his own bastardized holiday rhyme:
'Twas the night before
    Christmas and all through
    the ghettos,
the Afros were flashing their
    brand-new stilettos.
Then suddenly came flying
    through the night on his
    sleigh,
Old St. Nicholas. Could he
    save the day?
He looked those Niggers and
    Jews in their blood-shot
    eyes
and said, 'Hey there, boys,
    I've brought a surprise.'
Soon the whole crowd did
    tremble in fear,
for out of his bag, a cross did
    appear.
He pulled off his cap and
    there on his head,
that dreaded white peak sat
    there instead.
He spoke aloud with pride and
    no fear,
'You traitors have had it. The
    Klan is now here.'

The audience brings gifts too—in this case, a horse brush for these horses' [bleep].

For once something gets toppled other than a *Springer* guest, as reformed Klansmen Johnny Lee Clary fells the offensive tree.

Born Again?

Can these bigots change? The next guest proves that even the most closed-minded person can open his heart to love. Johnny Lee Clary is a former Imperial Wizard who has since written a book, *Boys in the Hoods*, renouncing the Klan.

Johnny Lee: **First thing we've got to do is get rid of this right here. This is the most offensive.** (He throws down the swastika-topped Christmas tree.)

J.D.: **No Christmas spirit! Man of God, acts of violence are all cut from the same cloth!**

Johnny Lee says he doesn't feel animosity towards these racists. **"When I see these people, I realize they're mentally ill. I used to be that way. I was sick. You don't want to hate a sick person, you want to help the sick person get better."** Johnny Lee says he was redeemed when a black man reached out to him with love despite all Johnny Lee's race-baiting. He quotes from the Bible, **"From one blood God made all races."**

Gifts from the Audience

It seems that audience members have brought the Klansmen holiday tidings of their own:

• A black Ken and a white Barbie doll. For, as the giver says, **"When God made man and woman, he did not distinguish what color."** (Taking the gift, Vince snaps the head off the Barbie, retorting, "Hey, Jerry, if that was O.J. and this was Nicole, her head would be broke off.")

• *The Diary of Anne Frank.* **"Anne Frank as a child was more of a woman than any of you-all will ever be men."**

What's It All About, Jerry?

"Some of our guests today saved their most venomous remarks for blacks and Jews, but those who they insult most with their diatribes are white Christians, by muddying and destroying the purity of Christmas's message. What today's guests painfully remind us is that in God's eyes, we are not defined merely by what we call ourselves or what holidays we choose to celebrate. We are what we are based on how we behave and believe the rest of the year when there are no holidays and nobody's watching but God.

"Till next time, take care of yourself and each other."

"Six years ago when your son was born, he had no prejudice in his heart."

I Need to Tell You This!

*A*nd this. And something else, too. There are revelations aplenty in this close-up look at a veritable love pentagon! Things start simply enough: Taurus is engaged to Raeleen, but he needs to tell her that he hasn't been faithful, even if it ruins their relationship. As this complicated web of deception and sexual peccadilloes unfolds, we learn that Taurus is quite an active bull, and he's far from the only one. But it gets better—there are distant cousins, long-term friends, and an unwanted baby all thrown into the mix.

Aired February 2, 1996

"Yes, it's another public service here on the *Jerry Springer Show.*"

The First Confession

"I've been a real dog."

Taurus is an articulate young man who appears well-intentioned. He's due to marry Raeleen next month, but he can't go through with it until he comes clean with her. **"I've been living a lie,"** he tells the audience. For five months he has been having an affair.

Taurus: **I've been a dog.**

Jerry: **Who have you been a dog with?**

Taurus: **Raeleen's best friend. Her maid of honor at the wedding.**

Jerry: **So not only have you been a dog, but her best friend has been dogging her as well.**

Taurus: **Yeah. She ain't no good either.**

Taurus knows he's in the wrong, but he's quick to share the blame. Apparently his fiancée shared details of his bedroom prowess with her friend, **"so it's kind of Raeleen's fault."** Monica decided she had to experience it. **"She was throwing herself at me,"** Taurus says, flagrantly **"dropping things and bending over"** in front of him. (Jerry deadpans: **"Well if you drop something it's kind of hard to pick it up without bending over."**)

Taurus is engaged to Raeleen.

Raeleen comes onstage to hear Taurus's confession. Beaming at first, she sits next to her man. Taurus gets right to the heart of the matter: **"I still want to get married, but I don't know how you're going to react to this. I've been sleeping with someone you know for five months."**

Raeleen's smile evaporates. She sits speechless. Finally she asks who it is, and Taurus tells her it's her best friend—who we learn is also his half-cousin! A class act all the way, she tells Taurus she is angry that he kept it a secret for so long.

But he's been having an affair with her best friend, Monica.

The Other Woman

When Monica enters she walks hysterically toward Taurus. She tries to hit him but is restrained by no fewer than five security men. Between her cracking voice and all her bleeped-out epithets, we can't understand exactly what she is saying. But we get the gist: She is furious!

Monica is more composed after a commercial break, but no less angry. **"He's trying to blame everything on me, like it was all my fault."** She says

Notable Numbers

- **1 (honorable guests on this show)**

- **3 (people Taurus has been involved with simultaneously)**

- **0 (lovers he will have now)**

And he's also been sleeping with his buddy Treynae.

"I'm trying to be nice but this is awfully sick."

Meanwhile, Monica is carrying...

Treynae's baby.

And Treynae's got another steady...

...Rufus.

Taurus was the aggressor, although Jerry helpfully points out that she never said no.

Now Taurus says he doesn't want to go through with the wedding to Raeleen. **"I love you as a friend, but not as no wife."** Yet he doesn't want Monica, either. **"I don't want nothing to do with her period, because you're just a little ho. She ain't nothing but a troublemaker."**

But this show's surprises are far from over, as Taurus indicates, **"I've got somebody else, too."**

The Other Man

Out struts a man in dreadlocks and dark glasses. Treynae has been Taurus's best friend all his life—and unbeknownst to his two women, Treynae has also been something else. Monica jumps out of her chair shrieking (as we'll soon find out, she's got even more to be surprised about than Raeleen, who looks like she's going to throw up).

Taurus and Treynae have been lovers, and not for just five months, but for five years, predating his courtship with Raeleen by a year a half. Did she ever sense anything? **"I suspected that his friend was kind of fruity, that's all."** For his part, Treynae never thought much of Taurus's woman: **"I told him don't marry the ho. I got so much dirt on Raeleen...."**

But that's not all folks. Monica reveals a bombshell of her own: She's pregnant with Treynae's child. **"You better be prepared to pay child support,"** she shouts. Treynae denies paternity, but admits they had a quickie after they both got drunk at a party. **"I just got in and got out. That's all that was."**

Yet Another Man

Now Treynae, too, has something to reveal. When Taurus got engaged to Raeleen, Treynae got himself **"a security blanket."** Out prances Rufus, a Prince-like clone in a shaggy black wig and a sequined jacket. The women are even more mortified, if such a thing is possible. As Rufus swivels his hips, Monica shrieks: **"My baby's marked! My baby's marked!"**

Girl Talk

Jerry clears the stage except for Monica and Raeleen. Monica cries: **"I'm so sorry. I'm so sorry. I don't want to lose you as a friend."** Replies Raeleen: **"You never really lost me as a friend. I lost you as a friend."**

Cheers

When Raeleen answers how Taurus could have let the wedding plans get so far: "Because he's stupid."

Jeers

When Taurus answers: "You're stupid, because you didn't know."

Six degrees of Taurus.

The third degree from Treynae.

Two former friends.

Treynae Sets us Straight

Before the show ends, Treynae wants to **"read all the books"** and goes person by person with his pronouncements:
**"To Rufus, don't go falling in love because I'm promiscuous.
"To Raeleen, I'm sorry if you couldn't satisfy your man but he found something else in me. ("I guess everybody found something else in you!"** she replies.)
**"To Taurus, you wasn't bringing the goods home, you couldn't satisfy me good enough, so I had to come get Rufus.
"And to Monica, you better come find me in Bolivia somewhere because I ain't raising no kid."**

Taurus admits that what goes around comes around. **"Treynae's just a ho, like I'm just a ho."** Jerry asks Taurus which of this motley crew he would choose if he could start over. After a long pause he confesses: **"I would like to be with Raeleen, but I know she don't want to hear this."**

What's It All About, Jerry?

"Why do people want to fly halfway across the country to tell someone they're living with a deep, dark secret for the nation watching? Perhaps there's an explanation: It's often easier to reveal something of discomfort to a nation of strangers than it is to someone you're intimate with. Those who use our show to dispense bad news must know that when the show is over the crowd and cameras both go away. Then it's just you and the person you hurt back home in real life. Television can do many things, but it cannot save a relationship; nor provide an easy way of getting out of one.

"Till next time, take care of yourself and each other."

"Was it worth losing Raeleen for fruit of the loom over there?"

Jerry Rescues
an Obese Man

enny Welch weighs 860 pounds. He no longer fits out the doors of his house, which really doesn't matter, because he can't get outside anyway—the bones and muscles in his legs and back are no match for his girth. Once a svelte and happy 600-pound Ethel Merman impersonator, and a frequent *Springer* guest, Denny is now utterly bedridden. He begs the *Jerry Springer Show* to save his life. In this episode, the show does just that by calling in a platoon of assistants ranging from building contractors to paramedics to city employees to doctors and nurses—all to put Denny back on the road to a sustainable weight. Can they save Denny? And is Denny finally ready to save himself?

Aired November 4, 1996

This Is No Life

Thirty-six year old Denny has been bedridden in his small-town Ohio home for the past month, weighing, he guesses, somewhere between 800 and 900 pounds (no conventional scale can hold him). He talks to Jerry while lying naked on his bed, covered in part by a large orange blanket.

Denny tells Jerry that his weight has begun to truly weigh him down. He details his dreary, horizontal days: A home health aide and a nurse come to help him wash, shave, brush his teeth and handle most other bodily functions, all from his bed. **"I go to the bathroom right here from my bed,"** Denny says. He tells Jerry that before the last month he did get around, by scooting in a chair, but the chair finally busted underneath him. Adding injury to that insult, the metal from the chair pressed into his chest as it collapsed, leaving a large scar.

But still Denny eats. **"I snack, bad,"** he admits to Jerry. Is food an addiction? **"When I get depressed, I eat a lot. The depression makes me eat."** Jerry wonders how he let it get this far. **"Why didn't you say way back when you were 400, 500, 600, 'I want to live. And every time I put those donuts or those potato chips in my mouth, that is killing me. I'm not going to do it'?"**

Ironically, it's his ballooning weight that has him most dejected. **"My life is not going anywhere. I used to do shows, I used to travel around the country. And now I'm here in my bed, and it's just like I'm dying here."**

Jerry wonders if Denny is finally serious about changing: **"We're going to tear down a wall, get you to a hospital, the doctors are going to treat you. They're going to put you on some kind of program. Why are you going to stick with it this time?"** Denny tearfully answers, **"Because I want to live. I'm tired of depending on people for things."**

The Many Faces of Denny

His first *Springer* appearance, as "Eartha Quake," in 1991.

Four months later: "The doctor said I wouldn't live to be 30, and I'm going to be 32 this year. A doctor's not God. They can't predict when you're going to die."

Six months after that he notes that one of his biggest problems is finding clothes and chairs to fit him when he travels.

As of 1993, Denny was not concerned with dieting: "Right now I'm using the weight as an advantage for my career."

A year later, ever-growing, Denny's health is starting to decline.

As of recently, Denny's become too large to leave the house.

The wall comes down.

Denny is lifted up.

And moved out.

Will He Ever Change?

Denny has been on *Jerry Springer* eight previous times, beginning five years earlier when he was a lithe 600-pound entertainer. Jerry plays clips from some of those appearances, and Denny cries as he watches. **"It hurts to see it."**

Meeting the Crew

Jerry stands outside the home with contractor Robert Jackson. Robert has taken down many walls before, but never to rescue an obese man. He explains the rationale: **"We couldn't get Denny through any of the doorways inside the house, so we decided to come through this way."** In the background, Robert's men remove Denny's bedroom window, saw through the drywall, and get ready to knock out an 8'x 8' section. The men are also building a deck, so the paramedics can hoist Denny out to the waiting ambulance.

Twelve Hefty Men

Jerry next talks to Joe Johnson, the man in charge of the 12 body builders from a nearby gym who will do the actual lifting. **"Obviously, we were concerned about his safety as well as our crew."**

Medical personnel take Denny's blood pressure and vital signs, dress him in a mammoth hospital gown, and—with heroic struggle—succeed in rolling a blanket underneath him for the paramedics to grab hold of.

Meanwhile, the men who will do the lifting mentally prepare themselves. One man warns the group, **"Don't drop it once we've got it."**

And the Wall Comes Tumbling Down

Jerry gives the command to take down the wall. Next he directs the ambulance to back up to the platform. But then he moves aside; he's not about to help lift Denny into the vehicle. Because no stretcher is strong enough to hold Denny's weight, the crew must carry him out on a door.

Time for the Weigh In

So how do you weigh an 800-pound man? Apparently, the way you weigh an 800-pound factory product: on an industrial scale. **"There were no other scales around that would weigh this much weight,"** a man explains to Jerry.

A worker provides the final numbers: **"Vehicular weight was 15,600; he grossed with the van and all at 16,460; his net weight is 860 pounds."**

At the Hospital

The ambulance then drives Denny to the hospital. An assembly line of people roll him onto a special stretcher. A man explains, **"We didn't have a table that could accommodate Denny, so through the courtesy of**

"This is it. No turning back from here. Once we tear down this wall, you're committed."

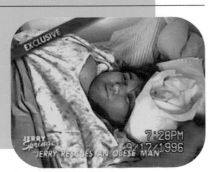

Glad to be back home.

the Cincinnati Zoo they afforded us an opportunity to use their polar bear table." The table, which itself weighs 400 pounds and can hold any animal up to 1,000, operates hydraulically.

Inside, Denny undergoes stress tests, and is pronounced surprisingly fit. He has no coronary disease. A relieved Jerry turns to Denny. "So far so good. OK? But no basketball till Thursday."

Next, Denny is loaded back onto the ambulance and heads to a diet clinic. The doctor and nurse interview him in the vehicle, since it would take another army to hoist him out. Their plan? Alas, no magic bullets. Denny must endure the same agony of every overweight American: diet pills, a strict eating plan, and exercise.

Homeward Bound

In the final segment the ambulance crew returns Denny to his house. He is overjoyed: "This bed is so comfortable. I am so glad to be home." As the ambulance drives away, Denny waves good-bye, the flesh still jiggling on his massive arms. We realize that he may have come very far, but he still has a tremendous way to go.

Jerry closes with a post-filming update. So far, he has lost 60 pounds, and the doctors are optimistic about his prognosis.

What's It All About, Jerry?

"There are a lot of people in America that have weight-control problems that really affect their health. And they can't wait for a television show to come to their house and tear down the side of the house so they can get the help they need. Each of us has to take control of our own lives. If we are eating too much, we have to have the will power to push away from the table, to start looking after our own health, to the exercise we really need. Take a look at yourself. If you need some help, save your own life.

"Till next time, take care of yourself and each other."

Backstage Secrets— Revealed!

While watching the seamless action of Denny's rescue makes it look effortless, countless hours by the show's producers actually went into the massive preparation. In addition to lining up all of the rescue personnel, it was the producers who had to find the equipment that would transport Denny to the hospital. For example, not only did they discover that stretchers and hospital carts don't handle so much tonnage—hence the use of the door and the polar-bear table— they also found that newer ambulance models are not up to the task. Producers made numerous phone calls until they located the older ambulance used for the job.

Jerry himself got into all sorts of hapless trouble during the shoot. We don't see it on air, but as he knocked out Denny's wall a small brick actually banged him on the head (he was a little startled— but fine). And while in the hospital waiting for Denny's test results, Jerry accidentally walked in on a nurse using the bathroom. They both shrieked and she ran from the room. Instead of being angry, however, she was thrilled to have met him!

Sadly, despite Jerry's efforts, Denny could not save himself. He passed away in 1998 at the age of 38. Jerry Springer helped to pay for the funeral.

The Mole People

ernard has lived in the train tunnels under New York City's Central Park for more than a decade. His neighbors are a married couple who have burrowed nearby for nine years. In a rare field trip, Jerry takes his cameras into their "homes." We see first-hand how members of an underground society eat, sleep, and pee in the dark, rat-infested squalor of an abandoned tunnel, and ponder why anyone would "choose" to live in what must be the dreariest place on Earth.

Aired November 15, 1996

Walden Tunnel

The eloquent Bernard often comes across as the underground philosopher. Here are his thoughts on living beneath the surface:

• "One has a tendency to associate darkness with danger, with despair, and it's quite the opposite. There's always light."

• "I'm not really a homeless person because I have shelter."

• "None of this junk is mine. Everything comes to Bernard. Don't you understand? I have to be dealt chaos."

• "Man's greatest fear is that he's always trying to defeat time. There is no time, really. It is ongoing."

"I believe there are probably people in this tunnel who aren't going to find a job anyplace. This is all they've got. And then I talk to you, and I've got to say, you can do better."

Bernard's Front Door

As the show begins we see Jerry walking with Bernard through beautiful Central Park. There is lush greenery all around, prompting Jerry to observe, **"You can't pay for a view like this."** But it's not a view Bernard has once inside his home. In fact, he has no view at all, for he lives far under the ground.

Bernard leads Jerry through an iron gate into a cordoned-off tunnel. Immediately, we are in total darkness. Jerry senses that musty, pissy smell **"which tells you, 'Okay, we're going underground for a while.'"** They walk down creaky stairs to the home Bernard has made for himself for nearly 11 years, stairs that transport Bernard from the cacophonous world above to a peaceful solitude below. That's how Bernard sees it, anyway. Jerry—and the rest of us—sees mostly garbage, dead rats, broken glass, and filth.

The tunnel once served as home and storage area to Amtrak, but is now desolate. Trains, however, still run on the tracks that pass through the tunnel.

Passing through Central Park, to Bernard's place.

The gates of home.

Welcome to My Castle

Bernard stops near where two pans are cooking over a fire. **"You are at the grill,"** he tells Jerry, giving him the grand kitchen tour. **"This is my dining area, where I prepare all my food and basically wash everything."** Rusty pots and pans, dozens of used coffee cups, discarded buckets, and stacks of crumpled papers are everywhere. **"No disrespect, but I don't see a lot of washing,"** Jerry notes. Bernard says the items he currently uses are kept clean in drawers and cabinets; everything else has long been discarded, but never thrown away. Cleanliness is so important to Bernard that he brings buckets of water down from a nearby gas station and boils it. Even his squalid-looking toothbrush, he says, is sanitized before use.

Bernard stocks his food on a makeshift pantry of chipped shelves. With the rats running free, all of his food is canned and packaged. **"My favorite meal is Hillshire beef kielbasa sausage, home-fried potatoes, and salmon cakes."** Every now and then he treats himself to a steak.

When Mother Nature calls, Bernard heads for a selected area of the tunnel. Getting other mole people to cooperate in keeping this area even mildly sanitary proved a challenge, he tells Jerry, but one where Bernard, an articulate, persuasive fellow, finally prevailed. **"It's just a matter of going to urinate or defecate and taking a can, gravel, and covering it, and it was a battle from day one with people to see the significance of that. But they got it together."**

Bernard's bedroom is a 20' x 25' room behind a **"keep out"**

"This has been home for 10 years."

"Ah, here we have a train!"

Daylight provides a harsh look at life underground.

This would be the "dining area."

Kathy: "I used to make fun of people like this because I never thought it would happen to me."

Bernard offers his own epitaph: "Here lived Bernard, one man who dared to be himself."

warning sign. He doesn't want to show Jerry the inside, **"because it is my privacy,"** but describes it lavishly as a carpeted room with a bed, dresser, wicker chairs, and a futon couch

Does he entertain any women there? Bernard says he's now in his fourth year of self-imposed celibacy, but before that time he actually did bring companions to his dungeon!

Here Comes the Train

"I'm probably one of the only people on Earth that have a train going through their living room," Bernard tells Jerry proudly. Soon a train passes right through—in all its horn-blowing, ground-shaking glory. **"This won't wake you up in the middle of the night?"** Jerry asks, incredulous. Bernard admits that is a hazard of his lifestyle.

There are plenty of other hazards, too. **"It's very hard work to exist down here. People think it's very easy, but it's very difficult. I have to go out, regardless of the climatic conditions, and acquire what I need."** He has no electricity (**"There are a few people down at the south end who tap power, but I always felt as though that would be cheating,"** he explains), using oil lamps and candles to banish at least a bit of the blackness. With no heat, in winter the temperature in his room never rises above 30 degrees. How does he handle the frigidity? **"I usually take one thermos of hot tea and one of soup or stew to bed with me."**

The Neighbors

Probably the biggest problem for Bernard is the caliber of the others who choose life underground. Bernard once lived in a larger room nearby, but **"it was set on fire by a guy."** A few years ago, guys who were clearly from the wrong side of these tracks raped and sodomized a mole woman. And many of his neighbors are alcoholics and drug addicts. Bernard denies he is either, although he admits, **"Up to this very day, I imbibe much beer and fine wines,"** and that several years ago he did use crack socially.

All I Need to Know I Learned from *Springer*:

• People who live underground are known as "mole people." "Topside" is their term for life above the tunnels.

• 79 homeless people died on or near New York train tracks in 1991, most struck by trains as they slept on the tracks.

• New York City shelters must be really awful if people prefer rat-infested, dangerous tunnels to them.

• There actually are places even New York's Finest are afraid to go.

But there are some lovely people, also—people who are down here because they seemingly went to the front of the line when they were handing out hardships. Kathy is one such woman. She tells Jerry in her sweet, disarming style that she has lived with her husband in the tunnels for nine years, because it is the only place they could afford to go. As she rakes mounds of trash away from her front door and a rat runs nearby, she says: **"I've been going through the system my whole life and, you know, they suck. Eight years and 10 different applications I put through the housing department, and they did [bleep] for me."** Bernard may find solace in his hobo existence, but not Kathy. **"I wouldn't wish it upon anybody. Hey, anything happens to you down here, you got a long walk out of here."**

If You Can Make It There...

What did Bernard do before he moved so far downstairs? He doesn't say, although he alludes to spending some time in film school and having once been a model and a flashy dresser.

To earn money now (after all, those steak dinners cost money, even if the rent is free), Bernard collects cans for recycling. **"I'm up at 4:00 every morning."** In winter, he can earn $100 to $150 dollars a day shoveling cars out of the snow. While he says one must be strong for that kind of work, **"God has been most gracious to me."** Not the kind of talk you'd expect from a man without an electric outlet to his name.

But Bernard is full of such unexpected outbursts (see sidebar on page 56). His long bouts of solitude have provided time for much reflection, something he considers crucial to a fulfilling life. **"I will not be one of those men who will depart from this life and will never have known peace of mind."**

Jerry asks if during the decade he ever tried life in the sunshine. Several years ago he tried a single-room-occupancy hotel, **"only to discover**

there was more chaos there than I had in the tunnel." He soon moved back down.

But now he is ready to give it another go. **"My body is telling me it's time to leave: my joints, my knees, and stuff. You know how elderly people say, 'Oh, it's going to rain. My arthritis!' I know what they mean now."**

Good thing Bernard was ready. We are told at the end of the show that Amtrak closed the tunnels and forced out the mole people shortly after Jerry taped this. Kathy and her husband finally got their government assistance and now have a habitable place to live. Bernard, too, has an apartment.

What's It All About, Jerry?

"The people we met here today are not just underground but are also under incredible burdens. We still live in a country where there are more people than homes, more people than jobs, more people than opportunities for them to be better off. So rather than passing judgment on them, perhaps we as a community have to decide: Why can't we provide the opportunities that someone, when they go down in the subway, is merely going home, not being home?

"Till next time, take care of yourself and each other."

"Is that the freedom you have, that you look around here and you say, 'You know what? I've got nothing left to lose?'"

Shock Rock

Did you know there are rock bands who have sex onstage, pee on the audience, perform bloody rituals, and literally whip fans? Some of it is pure theater, but some of it pure vile—and in this bizarre episode we meet "stars" from both sides of the fence. One masked madman has a "rape rock" band that lives up to its moniker—even advocating the assault of minors. His outlaw position is easily dismissed, but the violent campy theater of the band Gwar is far more challenging. To heighten the drama, these three outrageous rock bands face off with their fiercest critics: moms.

Aired January 31, 1997

Laugh of the Show

As Gwar sits onstage in full regalia, Jerry quips: "For those of you viewing at home, if you just joined us, today's show is about the impact of inflation on the world bond market."

A good *Springer* lesson: Always watch out for guys in hoods.

Dominique "shows women how to be dominant and strong."

A rare *Springer* plug: for Dominique's album.

Raping Rocker

Jerry's first guest is El Duce, the leader of a "rape rock" band, The Mentors. El Duce wears a hood and a shirt with an obscene slogan (It reads to the effect of **"Rape 'em and kill 'em and rape 'em again,"** but the outrageous words are blurred for broadcast). Jerry asks El Duce to remove his mask, which he does momentarily, revealing his large bald head and sinister smirk.

Aiming to be extremely provocative, El Duce happily defends his brutality. **"A man joins a rock band for one reason only, and that's the groupies. And sometimes the groupies don't put out, so you've got to rape them and sodomize them."** He has been arrested for having sex on stage with minors, he admits—and he's damn proud of it. The girls want it, he contends: **"They line up by the dressing room."**

Dominique, a 20-year-old Mentors groupie and a shock rocker in her own right joins in. Her skin-tight black unitard makes Bat Girl's costume look baggy, and is accented by numerous face piercings. She defends El Duce: **"He calls it rape rock. If they're paying to go to a show called that, that's their choice."**

But she says her band, the Spo-It's, has a different—albeit equally demented—angle: She literally whips audience members onstage. As she points out later in the show, she takes great pride in the fact that the violence in her shows is real, unlike the campy violence that other bands offer. **"It's a wonderful rush. It's ecstatic."**

She's Not Amused

The next guest, Susan, is a mother who herself was the victim of a gang rape some 30 years ago. She fumes at El Duce for promot-

The Many Masks of Gwar.

In Concert with Gwar

Jerry became "an honorary scalp dog," as a Gwar member put it, when he attended the band's concert and joined the group onstage. Unfortunately, his appearance is brief, as he is quickly fed to a large green monster.

Jerry onstage with Gwar.

Jerry ingested by Gwar.

ing this kind of violence, blaming him for giving boys the impression that they can wantonly take girls' innocence away.

El Duce: **Well, girls shouldn't go out there advertising for it.**

Susan: **I wasn't advertising for it. I was only 12.**

El Duce: **Well, you've got to start sometime!**

Susan next turns her wrath on Dominique. **"What are you going to do when your little girl comes home to you crying one day and says, 'Mom, these boys raped me?' Are you going to go, 'Oh good. That's great. I had it happen to me, too'?"**

Dominique's boyfriend Rik stands behind his girlfriend. **"I think it's great. I introduced El Duce to Dominique when she was 16 and he's been the best thing for her career."**

Onstage with Gwar

Gwar is another popular shock rock group, and Jerry decided to check out their concert before this taping. He plays a video of excerpts from the show; we see kids being tossed around, people being pelted with water, fights breaking out—and that's just in the audience. Onstage, intergalactic aliens battle one another with whips, kicks, huge steel hammers, and unidentified spewing liquids. **"Blood"** pours from an alien's cut eye. A creature blows fire.

Back on the *Springer* set, Gwar comes onstage in regalia that gives a new wrinkle to the term **"heavy metal"**—they wear it. Why did they get into shock rock in the first place? Jokes a band member: **"We weren't talented enough to make it unless we wore these silly costumes."** Wisecracks are a big part of their act, but rape is definitely not, they declare.

Jerry: **OK. You're not into that. So there's no violence in your message?**

Gwar member #1: **It's not really a message.**

Gwar member #2: **It's more like a massage.**

Gwar member #1: **A violent massage.**

The sole female in the group, Sylmenstra Hyman says that women here are held in high regard: **"I am the goddess, and every male in the audience worships the ground I walk upon."**

"Or else she'll walk upon them," a fellow band member notes.

Backstage Secrets—Revealed!

Steve Wilkos often accompanies Jerry to out-of-studio events, so it was natural that he went to the Gwar concert. Both men and the camera crew had a great time, but all were shocked when the audience began throwing beer cans, ice, cups, and other garbage at Jerry as he made his stage appearance. "Apparently, that's considered a sign of respect," Steve shrugs. Both Steve and Jerry were good-natured about nearly all of Gwar's requests at the concert—save one. As Steve recalls, "They wanted to take Jerry down into the mosh pit, but I emphatically said no."

This Mom's No Fan

Next up is an articulate—and hip—mother, Lisa, who is upset that her 14-year-old son adores such a violent band: **"It looks all real cute and fun, but why do you have to portray such a negative influence for the youth, for my kids?"**

Gwar member #2 (pretends to be crying): **I'm sorry!**

Sylmenstra Hyman: **It's only because we're out there fighting all the injustices that we see in society. All kinds of injustices, like child pornography, rape, drugs, censorship...**

Gwar member #2: **Republicans.**

Lisa is not amused. **"What about the portrayal of you ripping a fetus out of a pregnant woman? What kind of image is that going to have on my children?"** The band defends their concert, claiming that the evening news, TV dramas, and even football are much more violent, and that Gwar's violence takes the form of parody.

Shaun Loves 'Em

Teenage son Shaun comes out and genuflects before Gwar. **"They're the greatest band that has ever walked the face of this planet,"** Shaun glows, **"because they're creative and because they stand for the things that they stand for."**

Gwar's violence doesn't bother Shaun, although he's no fan of El Duce's: **"This guy's an idiot."**

So what's the pleasure for Shaun of attending a Gwar concert? **"It's the rush that you get. And the release that you get to do whatever you want."** Shaun denies that the band fosters violence (causing a Gwar member to humorously wonder, **"Where have we gone wrong?"**). But Lisa disagrees. Lisa: **He came back from that concert thinking it was OK to beat the crap out of somebody.**

Shaun: **I thought that before I even liked Gwar.**

As the program ends, Gwar members rise and perform a mock battle on each other. The audience cheers on the exciting action.

What's It All About, Jerry?

"Every generation seeks an outlet of defiance in its music. In fact, it could well be argued that art, no matter how outrageous, is the safest of all outlets for whatever ails a society at a given moment, and better that anger be expressed in a song than on the streets; better with a guitar than a gun. A child who has been taught values won't be swayed by a song, only by its rhythm.

"Till next time, take care of yourself and each other."

"When I hear that you promote rape, that is not only thoroughly disgusting, but it can't possibly be viewed as entertainment."

My Girlfriend's a Guy!

oday's guests are ready to spill secrets—the biggest one being that two of these very lovely looking women are actually men. And their boyfriends have no idea. But of course nothing is ever that simple. You'll learn who stays, who walks, and who's already out the door. And you'll learn a lot more about gender bending than you ever expected.

Aired February, 24, 1997

Brittany's secret: She's a guy.

Coming Out

Brittany—who becomes so popular after this show she soon becomes a *Springer* regular—opens the show by telling Jerry she is here to finally come clean. **"I want to tell my boyfriend that I am a transsexual, a boy."** She and David have been together on and off for two years, steadily for the past seven months. She says they plan to marry shortly.

Jerry can't understand how she kept such a seemingly obvious piece of information from David for so long, but she says her conservative background gave her cover. **"I'm from the South, and my family believes you don't have sex before marriage. I told him, 'If you love me and understand, you will wait.' So he understood."**

Unbelievably, Brittany knew that she wanted to be a woman so early in life that she even wore women's clothing to high school—where she first met David. When she went to college, she planned to have a sex-change operation, and return, *voilà*, a full woman, never to tell David the truth. But her conscience got the best of her. **"I love him too much, and one day he's going to want a baby and I can't give it to him."**

Things got more complicated right before the show, however, when David's best friend Kevin accidentally let it slip that he and David became gay lovers two weeks ago.

David's secret: He's with a guy.

The secret kept from Kevin: He thought they had broken up before he took up with David.

He can't believe it.

You go—girl?

Really; he can't believe it. He asks "her" for proof.

Beaten to the Punch

When David joins Brittany, she slaps him in anger. "**I hate you.**" Unbelievably, despite the fact that she has deceived him for two years, Brittany is furious that David hasn't been totally truthful with her!

Brittany: **Why would you lie to me the whole time? You never told me you had a boyfriend.**

David: **You never asked me. And, you know, we're not having sex. What do you expect me to do?**

Brittany: **I could see if you said it was a woman, but a man?**

David's boyfriend Kevin emerges. He claims he didn't know he was two-timing Brittany, because David told him that relationship was over. Brittany is even more outraged. "**He told you it was over, but we was just at the store looking at my wedding gown?**" An embar-

rassed David buries his face in his hands.

Brittany also can't believe her David would have turned to a man for affection.

Brittany: **Everywhere we go, David says, "I hate faggots. I hate gay people."**

Kevin: **I ain't no faggot.**

Guess What, David?

Jerry urges Brittany to share her own secret with David. She blurts it right out.

Brittany: **I'm kind of glad that you told me this because I have a secret to tell you, too.**

David: **Which is what?**

Brittany: **I'm a man.**

The audience applauds Brittany's blunt confession, and David's equally dramatic reaction: He jumps up and must be restrained by stage manager Todd Schultz. "**You mean to tell me**

Gender-Bending Glossary

What's the difference between a cross-dresser and a transsexual? No, that's not the setup to a joke, but rather something senior producer Rachelle Consiglio had to contemplate to work on a talk show that frequently showcases the full range of gender confusions. "Before I came here, I didn't know the difference, but they're very touchy that you use the right terminology about them"

Here's what Rachelle, along with devoted *Springer* fans, have learned:

- **Drag Queen:** A man who dresses as a woman occasionally, usually for a performance.
- **Cross-dresser:** Someone who finds it a sexual turn-on to dress as the other sex, an activity usually limited to the bedroom.
- **Transvestite:** Someone who prefers dressing as the opposite sex but doesn't want to physically change their gender. (Male transvestites generally consider themselves a "he," not a "she.")
- **Transsexual:** Someone who feels their natural gender is a mistake and wants to completely rectify the situation via hormones and surgery. Pre-operation transsexuals haven't yet gone under the knife while post-op transsexuals are as close to their adopted gender as they're ever going to get. (Unlike transvestites, male transsexuals, like Brittany, generally consider themselves a "she.")

Erica: a stunning . . . man.

Chris: a stunned man.

How did you get those boobs?

Pal Donna says the real boobs are the boyfriends.

you brought me all the way to Chicago to tell me that you're a [bleep] freak?" Clearly wanting no part of this circus, Kevin quietly walks offstage.

After David calms himself, he comes to a wacky but somehow reassuring realization about his own sexuality. **"So for the past two years I've been gay, so what's the problem with me being with Kevin?"** (Technically, he hasn't been gay with Brittany; as a pre-op transsexual [see sidebar on page 65 for a helpful glossary of relevant terms] she's now more woman than man.)

Jerry wonders whether in retrospect the men can see any clues that were telling. Kevin was suspicious of Brittany's deep voice—and even shared his insight with David once. But David just shrugged it off.

David: **I don't know any guys that go to high school dressed up like girls. And she always wears tights. You never see nothing! Two years and I haven't seen it? Where is it? Where is it?**

Jerry (feigning ignorance): **Where is...the high school?**

David: **No. Where is her [bleep]?!**

The Other Man in "Her" Life

Amazingly, Brittany isn't through with her announcements. She points to a man in the audience and announces that he is her new steady beau. **"We're getting married,"** Brittany joyfully exclaims. (She sure is planning a lot of weddings—none of which, we learn when she returns in future episodes, ever took place!) Jerry rushes the mike over to Rodney, who says he couldn't be happier. What does he find most attractive—that she's a man or a woman, Jerry wonders. But Rodney says he's most hooked by **"her personality."** Meanwhile, Brittany's betrayed beau David has heard quite enough, thank you. He proclaims, **"I'm leaving the show."** As he walks out his final words are, **"[Bleep]ing freak."**

Dishonesty Is Her Policy

In this next segment, we meet Donna, a buddy to another transsexual, Erica. Donna says her friend often keeps her gender identity from the men she meets, and that creates trouble.

Donna: **Erica has a problem of not telling them what she is. And then when the problem arises...**

Jerry (laughing): **That's probably when they know!**

Her sensuous friend Erica comes onstage, wiggling a more shapely body than even Donna's. With her full breasts, petite waist, and womanly lips, Erica undoubtedly gets catcalls whenever she sashays down the street. Erica says she doesn't tell most men she dates about her true gender because she wants them to want her for who she feels she is, **"and not for what's between my legs."**

Surprise! I'm Really... Eric?

Before Chris comes out to hear the bizarro news, Erica tells Jerry that it's really no big deal, because she can give Chris or any other man everything he wants. Brittany's still stunned ex-beau David (who returned to the stage) chimes in: **"You can't give him kids,"** before adding, **"You can give my sister some kids."**

When Chris comes out, Erica pecks him on the cheek. Chris looks like a really sweet guy   the kind any mother would welcome for dinner. He says the two have been dating for the past three months. **"I care about her a lot."**

Erica takes his hand in hers and begins rubbing it gently. There is something she wants him to know. His smile fades to a look of concern. Erica's voice breaks as she tearfully confesses.
Erica: **I'm a transsexual.**
Chris (laughing in disbelief, then widening eyes in a fit of nervousness): **You're a man?**
Erica: **You know that I'm a long way from being a man, but yeah, I haven't**

had the total surgery.
Chris: **How'd you get them** (pointing to her breasts)**?**
Erica: **I grew them.**

Chris clearly had no idea. He and Erica even slept in the same bed together—obviously they had just slept!—and still he couldn't tell. He is angered and betrayed. **"I feel like everything we used to talk about, like babies and all that stuff, was fake."**

Erica laments the sad life of a transsexual. **"If I get a sex change or not, these people out here are still going to see me as a man, just a man with a [bleep].** (Weeping) **In the past, when I have told some men, the first thing they say is, 'Oh, are you going to give me some oral sex? Are you ready for...' you know? No matter how feminine you become, what you do as a woman, you're still going to be a man."**

What's It All About, Jerry?

"There's no point in being judgmental here. You don't really understand a man until you've walked a mile in his shoes, even if they've got high heels. But by the same token, those who are now in a dress, even though they were born as men, have the moral responsibility of being understanding as well. As soon as it becomes clear that the person they're dealing with is starting to have some interest, I think they have a responsibility to tell this person that what he sees isn't necessarily what he gets. A girlfriend who isn't honest is neither a girl or a friend.

"Till next time, take care of yourself and each other."

"You've been together on and off for two years, and he doesn't know you're a guy? Did it just never come up in conversation?"

67

My Sister Stole My Husband

Lisa's husband Eldon is having an affair—and his mistress is Lisa's kid sister! Of course he's still sleeping with Lisa, too, and she wants him back if he'll end the affair. But Eldon is miffed at Lisa for a previous affair of hers, and he intends to stay with "Auntie" Gina. There's temper aplenty in this couple, and Gina's got her own beef with her husband Greg. When the hotheads have settled and the show comes to an end, there's a marriage license in shreds on the floor.

Aired May 8, 1997

"Why wouldn't you say to Eldon, 'Eldon, I don't care what your feelings are, this is my sister. Don't even come near my bedroom!'"

Twisted Sisters

When Lisa first appears, she portrays herself as the wronged wife. She and her 30-year-old husband, Eldon, have been together for 12 years, married for 8. They have three children. For the past four months, however, Eldon has been sleeping with both Lisa and her 18-year-old sister, Gina. (Gina, also married, has one child.)

Lisa says that first Eldon told her he was in love with her sister, but soon after said he wanted to try again with her. **"But he's sure not showing it by being with her still,"** Lisa says. **"I'm here today for him to make his decision."** What does Lisa now think of her sister? **"She's a slut, and as far as I'm concerned, I don't have one."**

Gina comes onstage and demands that Lisa **"tell them the truth."** A more complicated picture emerges. Lisa retorts, **"So what if I've had an affair twice?"** Lisa thinks she should be absolved because she feels very sorry for what she did, while Eldon and Gina do not. Gina demands that Lisa reveal more.

Gina: **She's making herself out to be this perfect angel.**
Lisa: **No, I've said I've cheated.**
Gina: **Why don't you tell them what you did?**
Lisa: **I said I cheated on him twice. I said that.**
Gina: **With who? With who?**
Lisa: **It doesn't matter who it was with.**
Gina: **Yes, it does. Yes, it does. This story, it does.**
Lisa: **This story has to do with you, bitch.**

Welcome to the Family!

Eldon appears and declares his devotion to Gina. Lisa is visibly hurt. Eldon admits **"it ain't right,"** but he says Lisa put him in this position. First, she went and had this fling on him. Then, **"every day for at least a year while we all lived in the same house together, she blamed me for cheating on her."** For some unexplained reason, the affair caused them to move in with her parents, where Gina was also living. The temptation to dip his ink in the family well apparently proved too great to resist.

Gina is eager to slam her sister if it defends her man.
Gina: **Look at the way she cheated on him. She didn't tell him.**
Lisa: **Would you shut up? This is**

One man, two sisters.

Lisa's had enough.

Greg's had enough, too.

And here are our final pairings.

See Eldon run.

See Eldon run fast.

See Eldon tackle Greg.

about you two, not me. You slimy slut. [Lisa tries to get up, but she is reprimanded by a security guy to stay in her seat.]

Gina : Yeah, stay in your seat.

Lisa: You're still the little one, let's remind you.

Gina: She didn't tell him about the affair. He found out.

Eldon: Yeah. A year later. Whenever she was pregnant. I got an almost 2-year-old little girl that I still ain't for sure if it's my child.

Lisa is happy to get a paternity test before he starts paying his child support, **"because I'm going to rack your ass."**

The Little [Bleep]

Let us not forget that Gina is also married, to Greg, a man Eldon calls **"a little [bleep]."** **"He's more of a man than you'll ever be,"** Lisa retorts.

As Jerry says, **"Let's bring him out,"** Eldon takes off for Greg's ass. The men scuffle, before security gets Eldon into a wrestler's hold on the floor.

When everyone is calm, Greg refuses to sit by his adulter-

"Why would you ever let him back into the bedroom after he slept with your sister?"

ous wife. He slides his chair far across the stage. In response, Gina pulls her chair closer to Eldon's so they can snuggle. An angry Lisa pushes her chair far across the stage to the left. The audience cheers the rearrangements.

Now Greg plays the innocent. **"See, look at this. I come on TV and I get slammed, and I ain't slept with nobody."** Greg thought he was happily married, but Gina quickly depicts a far different scenario—one that includes Greg's calling his then-pregnant wife **"every word in the book,"** and staying out till the wee hours of the morning. Greg's defense? **"I was immature."**

Eldon and Greg continue to argue, but as Eldon leans back on his chair, it promptly topples over, sending him to the ground.

Blood Bond

Eldon's sister Karla comes out. **"I've told both the women they're ignorant. I've told them all they're stupid."** While Karla thinks the promiscuous pair should wait for their respective divorces before getting together,

See Greg get rescued.   See Eldon in a headlock. Bad Eldon.

ultimately **"I think whatever makes my brother happy, that's what he should do."**

Intimate Strangers

Lisa tearfully tells Eldon that she **"hopes you guys will be very happy together."** But she is not ready to admit defeat. She tells Eldon how much their kids' hearts will be broken. He displays real emotion, too, but it's clear this marriage is over. Once again, he says none of this would have happened if she hadn't done what she done. As two-timing *Springer* men go, he stands as one of the more genuine, if still deeply twisted.

Finally, Lisa warns that Gina better not have a role in raising her children, **"or my ass is gone with my kids."** She laments the possibility that the pair might have their own children. **"They will be our children's cousins and their brothers or sisters!"**

The Final Free-For-All

Everyone is back and Jerry asks Eldon why he is so mad at Greg. He says Greg ignores his own baby. "You're white trash, brother," Eldon charges. Greg reaches into his pocket and pulls out his marriage license. **"I'm finished with you, man. Forget it,"** he says to Gina, as he tears the paper to shreds.

What's It All About, Jerry?

"Surely, it's not unusual for sisters to be attracted to the same person. Indeed, rivalry is a part of being a sibling. But what we've seen here today goes beyond friendly competition. There seems to be a total lack of respect, no care about hurting, embarrassing, or humiliating a sister, thinking instead only of number one. Maybe this could be remembered: Beware of someone who would backstab their own sibling to be with you. You should be more cautious than flattered."

"Till next time, take care of yourself and each other."

See Eldon...   go...   boom.

I Cut Off My Manhood

I n a show that Jerry, who has seen it all, calls **"absolutely astonishing,"** we meet Earl Zea, who chopped off his penis with gardening shears. He says he was driven to this dramatic act by Ronnie, a cat-killing, binge-drinking gay man he claims has been stalking him for years. Speaking out—and confronting Ronnie—for the first time since the incident, Earl admits he was out of his mind that night. Harder to figure is what the real relationship was between Earl and Ronnie, who did live together but dispute whether they were lovers.

Aired July 14, 1997

"If you want to be on the *Jerry Springer Show,* you send us a letter. You don't have to cut off your organ."

He did it. Really.

The shears.

The fears.

Mission Implausible

Jerry opens the show by holding a pair of large pruning shears identical to the pair Earl used on himself. To prove this actually happened, he plays footage from a local TV news program. It seems a rash act, but Earl later admitted his pruning was so premeditated that he had fed his dog and bought a pack of cigarettes in anticipation of a hospital stay.

Jerry gets right to the question foremost on everyone's mind: Why? Earl's answer is that Ronnie has been stalking him for years, repeatedly propositioning him for sex. **"It was the only alternative to get rid of him. If my sexual organ wasn't there,"** Earl unbelievably figured, Ronnie would not want him. Alas, adds Earl, **"It didn't work. He's still coming around."**

Earl takes the audience through the fateful night. He used a tourniquette so he wouldn't bleed to death, iced his genitals to numb the pain, then sliced off his penis with the shears, which didn't get the whole job done: **"I actually had to use a pair of scissors."** He has only a vague memory of then flushing it down the toilet—he can't imagine what else he would have done with it—and driving himself to the hospital.

"Was there any time, when you started to get the tourni- quette, started to get the shears, when you said, 'You know what, this isn't the smartest thing to be doing. Maybe I shouldn't do this?'" Earl agrees he was nuts that night, but blames Ronnie for making him snap, **"because he's been on my butt, stalking me."** In his mind he actually saw Ronnie cut

The tears.

The sneers.

"Lesbo" buddy Sue says she saw them doing it.

Neighbor Jodie says he's stalking her, too.

Bob says his brother likes the ladies.

him, and that's what he told the police at first. **"It took me a couple of days before I realized that I had done it myself."**

Jerry suggests that there were better alternatives: calling the police, having Ronnie arrested, moving, or even beating Ronnie up. Earl says he had done all of those things to no avail. So what is it like having no penis? The studio audience gets to see actual "after" photos. The collective gasps, winces, and squirms speak volumes. Earl can urinate, and he experiences no pain. Surprisingly, he can still get aroused—and even have sex. **"Because of how much it was cut, when it's non-erect it doesn't look like there's anything there. When it does get erect I do have enough to have sex."**

The Culprit

In a high-pitched, squeaky voice, Ronnie challenges Earl's story. **"I've been with this man for five years, off and on, from New York State to Arizona, to California."** Earl denies a relationship, but does admit that he took Ronnie in when his family rejected him. (They met because Ronnie was his former girlfriend's brother-in-law.) Jerry asks if the two men were ever romantically involved.
Earl (vehemently): **No.**

Ronnie: **Yes, we were. It sure the hell wasn't roommates. I wasn't sleeping on a couch.**

Ronnie admits that he is an alcoholic prone to fits of rage. Earl charges that Ronnie once broke his car windshield, and even killed one of his cats.
Ronnie: **I did not kill it. I didn't know it was in the chair, underneath the cushion.**
Jerry (laughing): **You sat on a cat?**
Earl: **He came in my house at four o'clock in the morning and started throwing my furniture around. And the cat was inside my recliner.**

The Lesbian Buddy

Ronnie's pal Sue says the pair were lovers, and that Earl used to take Ronnie to dinner and tell him he loved him. Earl denies it all.
"You're a liar, Earl."
"And you're a lesbo."

Sue screams that her own sexuality is irrelevant. She ends the shouting with this observation: "**I got up to go to the bathroom and there they were on the living room floor on the mattress that I gave them.**"

The New Victim

Earl's neighbor Jodie enters shouts at Ronnie, "**Why the hell are you stalking me and my family? Leave me the** [bleep] **alone. I don't love you.**" It seems since Earl moved into his new apartment (in a futile attempt to hide from Ronnie), Ronnie has been knocking on Jodie's windows and demanding to move in. Ronnie denies everything, unless he "**was drunk and I don't remember.**"

The Loving Brother

Earl's brother Bob stands up for his sexuality. "**He gets along good with women. In the last year he's dated three different girls that I know of.**" Earl tells Jerry laughingly, "**I've even been hitting on some of your assistants back there.**"

The Audience Wonders

There's no shortage of questions from the audience (and surely you have your own). Audience member: **What did the women you've dated since the incident think about it?**
Earl: **I've only been with one woman since then, and she didn't hold it against me.**
Audience member: **Can you still have kids?**
Earl: **Yes, eventually, after reconstructive surgery, I will be able to have kids.**
To another question, Earl admits that while Ronnie and he never slept together, they did at least sleep "**in the same room maybe, but not in the same area.**"

The Medicine Man

At the show's conclusion, surgeon Lawrence Ross, M.D., describes the procedure for

"**Any straight man would not let that little freak get within 50 yards of them, let alone live in the same house.**"

reconstruction, where skin is grafted from the leg, arm, or abdomen. "**We can, for the most part, make a functional organ.**" As he explains, castration is actually more common than one might expect (though more often from industrial accidents than self-mutilation).

What's It All About, Jerry?

"**Certainly, to do what he did, no matter what the motivation, is a moment of insanity and yet, let's face it, if he had cut off his arm this never would have been a show. In a culture obsessed with sex, it's hard not to cringe at even the thought of someone slicing off that particular part. If we need to articulate a lesson here let it be this: If you want to cut a relationship, make sure its the relationship you're cutting off.**
"**Till next time, take care of yourself and each other.**"

"**I mean, wouldn't you rather live in Nebraska than cut it off?**"

I Have Many Lovers!

R ufus and Treynae are two colorful characters who are favorite *Springer* guests, and they unquestionably keep many lovers in play. In this installment, the two bisexual lovers—who swear they dress much more manly when they're out with women than the flashy costumes they wear today—come clean with their shocked women. And from the other side of the fence, a lesbian admits her infidelity to her lover, hoping to come away with a happy threesome.

Aired July 30, 1997

"Wait a second. I see you walk into the room and the first thing that comes to my mind is not, 'Gee, there's a straight guy!'"

A Gay Day

Treynae is good at striking poses.

So good that he's fooled Cheeta, and is himself a cheater.

She doesn't take it well. And she wants her pants back.

Rufus doesn't take the news about Cheeta well either.

Treynae prances onstage and strikes various female-model poses. His voice is as effeminate as his movements as he responds in soprano to Jerry's greeting: **"I'm doing good, girl. I mean Jerry. That always slips out."**
Jerry shows us clips from a previous episode featuring Treynae and his lover, Rufus, "I Want Your Man." It seems that Rufus is still in the picture, and will appear on the show later. Treynae says, **"I'm going to always love Rufus, but sometimes, I like [bleep]—okay, women—too."**
The woman of this hour is Cheeta, a bombshell so beautiful (**"she is all that"**) that Treynae tried, unsuccessfully, to make himself faithful to her. **"I started to change my ways. But that ain't going to never happen."** But Cheeta has no idea that Treynae is bisexual, and she knows Rufus only as one of her best friends—she's like a sister to him. How can this be? As Jerry puts it, **"When you first walk into the room the first thing that comes into my mind isn't, gee, there's a straight guy."** But Treynae swears that when he goes out cruising with Rufus you would think they are **"straight as boards."** He dresses and acts in a more manly fashion: **"I put on my jeans and whatever. I go up to the girl like [deepens voice], 'Hey.'"**

A Bombshell for the Bombshell

The shapely Cheeta talks lovingly about her nearly year-long relationship with Treynae. **"He's fun to be with. I can talk to him about anything. He's there for me when I need him."** Does she know why Treynae brought her here? **"We've been talking about marriage for a while, so...."**
Treynae then comes out to meet his lover. He crosses himself before emerging—and for good reason. **"I'm a clown today,"** he says to try and reassure her. (It turns out, amusingly, that he is wearing her tights.) But Cheeta is upset by his appearance. And then Treynae admits: **"There's a little bit more girl in me than you know. I'm bisexual. This is who I am. I love men."**
Horrified and humiliated, Cheeta smacks Treynae across the face so hard he falls over backwards onto the floor. The audience applauds her maneuver—and her dead-on aim. **"You**

Backstage Secrets—Revealed!

Viewers frequently call to inquire about favorite guests, even long after the program airs. Callers ask about Rufus and Treynae more than nearly anyone else.

As a result of the dynamic duo's many appearances other TV shows have called to book them. But so far they are loyal to *Springer;* they regularly call the producers to update them on their newest relationship configurations. So stay tuned, and you're likely to see these bisexual bedfellows again soon.

Juanitra is surprised by Rufus's revelation.

Straight pal Mike offers her himself instead.

Rhonda says it's hot with Lovette.

But that steam also fuels Lovette's temper.

know I like it rough but not like that. You're embarrassing me."

Cheeta can't believe this is the same man she has known.

Cheeta: **You're not bisexual! You're just gay!**

Treynae: **No. I'm trisexual. If I try it, I like it, I keep doing it.**

Cheeta: **That's not a word. That's a freak. Look at you. You look like a stone-ass freak.**

Then Treynae drops the second half of his bombshell, telling her that Rufus is his lover.

More Lovers, More Surprises

Out dashes Rufus, looking a lot like the Artist Formerly Known as Prince, and it becomes clear that he may soon be the Bisexual Formerly Known as Treynae's Lover. It seems Treynae hasn't told him about his relationship with Cheeta. Rufus jumps up to threaten Treynae, who pops up swinging, their girly fight coming across like a parody. **"Deal with it, little girl,"** Treynae says.

Rufus, too, has a girlfriend who hasn't been let in on his little secret. Juanitra comes out and is stunned by her man's over-the-top appearance. Rufus is blunt and brutal: **"The only reason why I'm with you is because of the sex. I don't like you."** When he tells Juanitra he is bisexual, she jumps up to slug him, but the security men quickly sit her back down.

Treynae's lifelong friend friend Mike joins the group and he, too, is shocked to learn Treynae has eyes for more than women. **"When we go out to clubs, it's like this** [pointing to his own jersey, khakis and baseball cap], **like me. Guys who go squeeze girls, talk to girls, do everything."**

Juanitra thinks Rufus is **"out of your mind,"** and she's not going to stand for this degrading treatment. **"When I get back, I'm calling my brother to beat your [bleep]."** Cheeta is also finished with her man. **"Baby, give me my walking papers today because you're out the door."** And it seems that Treynae may be dispatching Rufus. **"I'm done with him. I need to be by myself, because he's not helping me anyway."**

Lesbians Are Unfaithful, Too

The show now moves on to another vicious love triangle. First, we meet Rhonda, who has been with her lover, Lovette, for a year. They had previously agreed that it was OK to date other men, but not other women. Now Rhonda is secretly seeing another gal. She is worried about confronting Lovette because **"she has a very bad temper and kind of goes pretty crazy."**

When Lovette comes onstage the women are openly affectionate. They hug and lip-kiss; Lovette takes Rhonda's hand and licks it; Rhonda reciprocates. How would Lovette describe the relationship? **"Hot. Every day, every hour on the hour. It's all good."**

Rhonda turns to her loving lady and breaks the bad news. "**I met a woman a couple months ago.**" Lovette reacts by pulling Rhonda's hair, then choking her.

Sweet Georgia

Rhonda's new girlfriend, Georgia, comes out swinging for Lovette. Lovette grabs Georgia's golden locks tightly, even as the security men struggle to separate them.

Georgia and Rhonda join hands, further infuriating Lovette. "**Get you hands off her. Don't disrespect me because I'll kick your [bleep] again.**"

Rhonda reveals to Lovette the real reason she has wanted to introduce her women to each other. "**I showed Georgia your pictures, some of your shots.** [X-rated? We'll never know.] **And she was like, 'She's beautiful. Introduce me to her.'** "

Lovette is not interested in a threesome with the likes of Georgia. Lovette tries to kick her, but Steve Wilkos leaps in front of her. She tries to walk around him but Steve body-blocks again. The audience chants, "**Steve! Steve! Steve!**"

Lovette finally sits down and issues her ultimatum: "**You can have her if you want. Get the [bleep] out of my house. It's one or the other.**" Rhonda says since each is a gorgeous, sexy woman, it will be impossible for her to choose. "**I want both of you!**" But that seems like a distant dream.

As the credits roll, viewers are treated to an outtake from Jerry's closing comments. Lovette is putting a ring on Rhonda's finger and demanding, "**It's either her or me.**" As Lovette is lead offstage so Jerry can reshoot his closing, Rhonda keeps the ring on her finger, but then takes hold of Georgia's hand.

What's It All About, Jerry?

"**Dating around, developing several relationships, each with their own value, is not unnatural or even immoral. But what is wrong Is when one of your interests is led to believe that she's the only one. The point is if you're going to play the field, so be it. But let each of the players know there are other players in the lineup, also.**

"**Till next time, take care of yourself and each other.**"

Grabbing hair,

No threesome here,

How to choose?

OK, you lose.

Big-Busted Strippers

n a culture obsessed with big boobs, it was inevitable that some women would literally take it to the max. But even assuming for excess, the exotic strippers who prance and dance in this episode have bustlines that are nothing short of miraculous. In all cases, these are just about the biggest breasts that money can buy. These women say that turning men's heads (and having those heads crash into all manner of things from not watching where they're going!) offers delicious advantages, and that they can get away with anything. Even women love them, they claim, and they are backed up by a naturally well-endowed woman who wants to go for the gusto—over the objections of her man!

Aired August 7, 1997

The doctor brought Candy her apples. A view of the Andes. Was that Meshalynn or Megalynn?

Teeny Weeny Bikinis

This show opens with a video of the beautiful guests on the sand in Daytona Beach, Florida, where this episode was shot. When they turn to face the camera, we see a row of gigantic bosoms busting out of tiny bathing suit tops.

Jerry welcomes the women, all exotic dancers, to his poolside stage. They enter one-by-one, as if in a Miss America parody. In addition to their unusual physical attributes, they sport suggestive stage names, including Lisa Lipps, Honey Melons, and Candy Apples. Each introduces herself and explains why she loves her outstanding physique.

Living Extra-Large

Jerry plunges in to discover why these women keep seeking out surgeons. They say they enjoy the attention—and boy, they do get plenty of it. Meshalynn is proud of her mature body. **"Little girls have no [bleep]. Women have [bleep]."** To which one woman in the audience flashes her chest and proclaims, **"I'm not a little girl, but for my size I've got a nice pair of breasts."** Jerry thanks her **"for that magical moment."**

Three's a Crowd?

These women may love their big breasts, but their loved ones are perplexed. Meshalynn's pal Neva thinks she has gone too far. **"Large is underspoken. This is nasty."** The women quibble over who has the better figure. Neva: **It's a waste.**

Meshalynn: **It's a woman.**
Jerry: **Is that a woman, or is it silicone?**

Candy Andes's man Kelly also has his gripes: **"Well, I think they're nice to look at and they're damn near perfect, but there's one minor detail they left out. They're absolutely fake!"** He can't even figure out how to react around such unnatural wonders: **"I don't know whether to caress them or kick the tires!"**

Crystal Storm's friend Beth agrees it's nuts. **"I see them getting in the way all the time. She can't see her feet, and can't do anything by herself."** Jerry wonders if Crystal can tie her shoes. **"Not when I'm standing up."**

An older woman in the audience declares, **"When you get older, you're going to sag like balloons that are starting to go flat."** No way, says Candy Andes: **"When I start sagging, I'm just going to keep getting them bigger and bigger and pick up all the loose skin. They defy gravity."** Candy even knows equally endowed women in their later years whose continued plastic surgery has kept them bountiful.

You Call Those Breasts?

Originally, the producers booked nine women for this show. Guests were asked to send in photos of themselves to document the huge sizes they had described on the phone, but the naughty ninth had never provided her evidence. When she showed up, it was apparent that her breasts, while big, just weren't humongous enough. It was no doubt the first time this big-bosomed woman was ever told she was too small.

Kayla's on fire.

It's a Crystal Storm.

Lisa does her dance.

Honey offers her melons.

Meet Erica—who thinks she's too small.

"I want those!"

Stop My Wife, Please

Next up is Dennis, a man whose wife, also a club dancer, wants to trade up from her own nicely endowed size to the likes of these women. **"I'm totally against it. It's a freak show."** Dennis' stunning wife Erica then enters, to the cheers of the crowd. She wears a tight orange dress showing off her terrific figure. But the gifts God gave her apparently aren't satisfying. She walks past the other women pointing: **"I want those! I want those!"**

Erica: **That to me is more eye-catching, and I just—mmm!—I like it.**

Jerry: **More eye-catching? So is a tattoo on your forehead!**

Dennis warns her not to do it, threatening, **"This is going to end the relationship."**

A Curious Audience

Audience members have some practical questions. What size were the women before their implants? A charming Minka offers her assessment: **"One size bigger than your head, baby."**

Where do they ever find bras? The women say they shop the same stores every woman does, although they do get some custom made.

Does it bother them to be the object of such ridicule? While all agree they don't

"It's absolutely gorgeous here in Daytona Beach. I want to stay forever. But I can't find a thong."

dress so provocatively when they're not performing, Lisa Lipps wants people to see beyond her blaring headlights: **"I think you should judge us on the fact that we donate a lot of money and a lot of time to disabled American veterans, the Shriners Children's Hospital, things for the blind. So I don't just use this for myself."**

Do a Little Dance

In the next segment the women give a little taste of what men pay top dollar to see in their clubs. The biggest cheers are reserved for cowboy-clad Candy Andes, who corrals friendly stage manager Todd Schultz to drop to his knees so she can **"ride"** him like a horse. Jerry can't resist: **"It was hard to tell what was the boob up there!"**

What's It All About, Jerry?

"To generations of a culture married to visual images, the centerfold of a young man's consciousness, particularly at an age where most consciousness is below his belt, is that picture of a big-breasted woman, the object of his desire. But the issue isn't breasts at all, big or small. The issue is that any particular body part is used to define a human being. And that is where disrespect and degradation of women begins. A guy who sees a woman only for her breasts is really the biggest boob of all.

"Till next time, take care of yourself and each other."

Big-Busted Bonuses

Some thoughts from the panel on why they cherish their ample assets:

• "I love my big breasts because they make me feel sexy."

• "I don't have to get in line for anything."

• "People part for me like the Red Sea."

• "I like my big breasts because they catch big checks."

• "Having big breasts is like possessing the big fruit of passion."

• "You can get away with a lot more. When they're so busy looking at these, you can be right over their head."

• "These are power. They're power."

Backstage Secrets— Revealed!

When *Springer* stage manager Todd Schultz was told to hang around during the dances in case he was needed, he wasn't surprised. "I'm like the show dork," Todd explains. "When something dumb or funny has to be done, I get called up to do it." The minute he saw Candy Andes in her cowgirl gear approach him, he figured this was it. Candy rode him like a horse—an experience so thrilling that he chose to make even more of it. "I'm thinking, this is America. I believe in equal rights, so I decided I was going to ride her like a horse, also." Candy had used Todd's belt as a reign, and Todd decided it would also make a terrific whip. He began lightly smacking Candy's bottom, but quickly realized she was wearing nothing but a thong. "I looked down and saw that her butt was getting a little red," he says. So does Todd's face as he recounts the once-in-a-lifetime experience.

A big round of applause for our horse.

Todd's back on top.

You Stole My Lover!

Ashley bitched.

T he fur—or hair—literally flies here, as jilted women confront the temptresses. Hair is pulled and a wig goes flying, and two mothers are brought into the fray (one of whom ignores Jerry and holds her own talk show). In the end, the men show more backbone than most *Springer* guys—each actually choses just one woman.

Aired September 29, 1997

Postpartum Blues

A shley sits on stage and tells her tale of betrayal. She gave birth to her boyfriend Steve's twins just one month ago (it's hard to believe, with that body). When she was five months pregnant, however, Steve left her. **"He said that since I was pregnant that I fussed at him all the time, that I just bitched at him"** (the audience roars its disapproval). To make matters worse, he left this mom-to-be for a professional stripper. After the babies were born, Steve asked to come back. But she says that stripper Sonia still won't leave him alone. Can Steve be faithful? **"I believe he could, if he tries."**

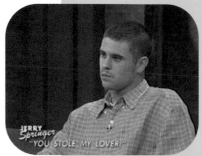

Steve bolted.

Slapped Around by Sonia

Steve emerges to the jeers of the audience. He is ambivalent when he says he came on the show to come clean, **"to just let both of y'all know**

Sonia strips.

"You're hiding behind the women, Steve. You're letting them fight when you're the culprit here, really."

And now Steve's bolting from her.

what's going on." He says he still loves Ashley, but when she demands that Steve kiss his new lover good-bye he doesn't respond.

Ashley is asked to go backstage so Steve can speak to the stripper. Beautiful blond Sonia's entrance elicits applause from the men in the crowd. Sonia has been with Steve for seven months and describes the relationship as **"great."** Steve looks her in her eyes and begins his confession, but until the words come across his lips we are not entirely sure which woman he will select.
Steve: **I still love Ashley. We've been getting along lately.**
Sonia: **And you've been sleeping in my bed?**

With those words Sonia starts swinging, and stays angry. **"She's stupid if she stays with you because once a cheater, always a cheater,"** Sonia says Steve has been pursuing her, and that he even stayed at her house this past week and proposed marriage. Ashley listens backstage and holds back tears. Steve replies, **"I was drunk."**

Here Comes Trouble

When Ashley returns she goes straight for a surprised Sonia and knocks her backwards over her chair. Ashley accuses her of being a low-life stripper and man-stealer. Sonia replies, **"I don't know why you came here putting me down. It was your man who was cheating on you."** Ashley issues her ultimatum to Steve: **"Either you tell her now, or I'm leaving this show without you."**

But the battle of the bitches isn't over. Sonia's gal-pal Terry comes out, dashes behind Ashley's chair, and yanks mightily on those carefully coiffed ringlets. Ashley challenges Terry to a fight back home. Terry is ready: **"Bring it on, bring it on. I'll stomp your ass."** Terry says she is pissed at Ashley for dissing her girlfriend, when Steve is the one who caused this mess, and maybe even Ashley herself. **"Evidently she ain't doing something right because he comes to Sonia's bed."**

So what does Steve—who has sat quietly in his chair the whole time the women battled around him—really want? **"I want to be with Ashley,"** he finally admits. **"Good thing, she can have him,"** Sonia declares. But will Ashley take him back? She pauses for a moment before tearfully saying, yes, **"I love him. I do."**

Springer Scoreboard	
First Lovers:	1
Second Lovers:	2

A Memorable Moment

When Victor's mother Vivian comes out, she goes straight to work lecturing her boy. Eventually Jerry manages to say hello—and she abruptly cuts off her tirade, flashes Jerry a smile, and shakes his hand. But then's she back to business, oblivious to Jerry and the studio audience.

85

Lubertha left home and lost her man.

Laquita came to Chicago...

...and lost her wig.

Victor's going home without her.

What's Love Got to Do With It?

Having been warmed up by this last tress-tangling trio, the audience is ready for the scorned lovers of the next act. Lubertha claims she returned from a trip—a **"two- or three-month"** vacation—to find that her boyfriend, with whom she shares three children, had moved a new lover in her home. **"I'm not leaving this show without my man."** What if her man really loves this other woman, Jerry wonders. Answers Lubertha: **"No, see it doesn't go that way. He's gonna come home whether he loves her or not. He's coming home."**

The other woman, Laquita, comes out and the bickering begins. **"It's over. He's mine,"** Laquita charges. **"She needs to butt her ass out, point blank,"** Lubertha demands. The back and forth becomes so intense that Jerry laughingly turns his head from side to side, as if watching a tennis volley.

Laquita tells us that Lubertha and Victor have been separated for 2½ years. Lubertha stands and retorts, **"No, that's off and on, because you keep coming into our life."** As she finishes these words she pulls Laquita's hair and bashes her with the bouquet. Flower pieces fly—and so does Laquita's wig!

Back in Action

After the commercial break, Laquita is back, both hairpiece and dignity somewhat restored. Her claims are bolstered by Victor, who soon appears. Victor contradicts Lubertha's assertion that she left for a short refresher. **"She went with some young mother[bleep] in New York. She called my mother and said, 'Yo, keep my kids. I don't want 'em no more. I'm out.'"** He says their relationship was over even before she left, when Lubertha went out to bars every night **"wearing them little hot slutty clothes."** Lubertha admits she was wild but insists she has changed now. But Victor's not buying: **"You're the past, girl. Laquita's the future. Bye, see you, take a hike, beat it."**

Lubertha's got one more wild card up her sleeve. Victor's mother, Vivian, walks in front of Victor's chair and proceeds to lecture him on why he should return to Lubertha, who apparently is living with her now. **"She's gone to church, got saved and all,"** Vivian tells him, and returning to her would be the right thing for the kids. Victor cheerfully points out that **"My mother's not with my father, so why should I be with my babies' mother,"** before declaring once again his choice of Laquita.

By the Numbers

3 (one-on-one chick battles)

2 (hairs mussed)

1 (wig lost)

Betrayed Donna and her mom, Sherri...

...are mad that Jesse wed her cousin.

The Final Confrontation

Last on the docket is Donna and her mother Sherri, who say Donna's relationship with her boyfriend Jesse was wrecked by her cousin Jill. **"She's a tramp,"** exclaims Donna. **"They've ruined my life."** Her mom agrees: **"She can't forget what the bitch did."**

Out prances Jill, who clarifies things by telling us says she's been happily married to Jesse for 1½ years and that she and Jesse have a son together. They just want Donna out of their lives. Jesse then comes out and agrees with Jill, telling Donna and her mom they're both nuts.

Jesse: **I used to support your family.**
Sherri: **Exactly. He was there all the time.**
Jesse: **All the time? I was only there after I drank a 12-pack!**

Without hesitation, Jesse selects Jill over Donna, planting a juicy kiss on her waiting lips.

What's It All About, Jerry?

"The truth is, when we fight to win back an ex, more often than not, it's either because we're lonely for the moment, or our ego can't stand the idea that he went for someone else. In either case, you deserve someone who by his own volition wants to be with you and only you, and doesn't need to be convinced.

"Till next time, take care of yourself and each other."

"You're saying you love Ashley and you want to go back with her, and yet three nights ago you proposed to Sonia?"

Klan-frontation!

"In this country, everybody's free. We even let people like you in."

7he sheets really hit the fan in this wild encounter between Ku Klux Klan members and the radical Jewish Defense League. Ostensibly this show will introduce us to new members of the Klan and Jerry will see if they can be dissuaded from joining the organization. Instead, the first portion of the show is a platform for these people to share their impassioned and contradictory views. Yet the animosity isn't even confined to throwing punches; epithets and put-downs are also continually hurled from under those white sheets towards black audience members, other guests, and even the Jewish Jerry Springer. And Jerry, under personal attack, takes a more active role in expressing his own views than in almost any other episode of the show. The Klan members are confronted, literally as well as verbally, by the leader of JDL as well as by some people from the audience. In the end, the KKK serves to prove that, yes, its members are indeed supreme—if only in their level of hatred and animosity.

Aired October 22, 1997

Misunderstood

Ku Klux Klan members Tonia and Jody enter chanting **"White power!"** to a chorus of jeers. Tonia has been a KKK member for four years and works hard to recruit others. Now she is saddened that her beloved organization is so misunderstood.

"You people only see the picture of the Klan that the Jew media puts out." Apparently the Klan is not about burning crosses and lynching people. Tonia sets us straight: the Klan is actually a very civic-minded organization, holding food drives and raising money for homeless white people. **"We believe in separatism, not white supremacy. That's where you got it wrong."**

So why not just stick with whites herself and let others live and let live? Because Jews influence others' thinking by commanding so much power in the world, she claims. Most ominously to Tonia, this Jewish cabal gives off terrifying messages through even the most innocent-seeming media.

Tonia: **You've got Barney out there, saying it's okay to interbreed with a chink, a gook, a nigger.**

Jerry: **This is the United States of America,** and in the U.S.A. we all belong, not just you.

Jody: **No. The pride stops when your group or any group comes in and demolishes a nation.**

Jerry: **You know what? The Native Americans were here first, so get your ass out of this country!**

Tonia: **You're a Jew. Why don't you go back to Israel!**

Jody decries the double standard whites like him are subjected to. **"If I stand up and say I'm proud to be white, I'm a racist. But any nigger stands up and says, 'I'm proud to be black,' then it's all right? That is wrong!"** To their thinking, they are not racist, and everyone else is. Jody tells Jerry: **"Are you proud to be a Jew? You're racist because you're proud of your heritage."** Jerry's reasoned response is, **"I'm only proud of things I can personally accomplish, or that people can personally accomplish."**

And even greater horrors are apparently out there.

Jody: **Where I come from, we see blacks standing out by mailboxes waiting.**

Jerry (feigning anger): **Oh! I hate that when other people stand by mailboxes!**

Jody: **They stand there waiting for their welfare checks. I go pick up my check from work.**

Tonia and Jody: just two civic-minded souls.

Proud of his race—the coneheads?

Party of five.

The audience chokes.

A mom gloats.

The Dragon blows smoke.

Rubin enters the lion's den.

He grabs for McQueeny's cynically-worn skullcap.

There's no exclusion here; everyone's in on the act.

Married, With Children

Jerry's next Klan guests were recruited in the past few months. Rocky and Sandy are married with three growing children, while Stacy arrives solo. All wear hooded robes.

Why join the Klan now? For the married couple, the reason is quite pragmatic. They have always been white supremacists, but only recently moved from the West Coast, where the Klan apparently doesn't operate. Though they talk of white pride, as Jerry points out repeatedly, **"You're not proud. You're covering yourself up."** (Sandy eventually takes her hood off; Stacy does not.)

The Dragon

Grand Dragon Mike McQueeney appears next. A race-baiter, he has long held controversial rallies around the country. He is ready with all kinds of explanations for what's wrong with our country:

• **"We're all white. Something that you, Jerry, know nothing about because you came from a Turkish Mongrel race, a tribe from the Middle East."**

• **"Jews were slaves 4,000 years ago, and niggers were slaves. And they're all still slaves."**

• **"When the Clinton Administration has a Jew on one side and a negro on the right, this is what's running this country. Alan Greenspan runs this country."** (Prompting Jerry to retort: **"Oh, so it's Alan. I thought it was Rabbi Clinton."**)

• **"The negroes are 200,000 years behind us in evolution. Look at the slope of their forehead and their protruding jaws. You look like a monkey, and that's what you are."**

He can dish it out, but can he take it? McQueeney appears wounded when Jerry, remarks, **"We're all laughing at you because we know you're stupid."** The Dragon replies, **"I don't call you names, Kike-boy."**

Fighting Back

The next guest, Irv Rubin, is the founder of the radical activist group the Jewish Defense League, introduced by Jerry as **"a controversial civil rights leader."** As soon as he enters a melee breaks out, with countless security men, bodyguards, Klansmen, JDL members, and even audience members up on stage throwing punches, chairs, and profanities.

Calm is restored only when everyone but Irv is led offstage. Jerry takes Irv to task for his violent tactics: **"That doesn't make you any better than them!"** Irv defends his actions: **"In my view, what goes around comes around. The bully picks on the guy who doesn't fight back."**

A Final Klanfrontation

Jerry still wants to see if there is any room for conversation between these two polarized groups. Tonia's father Jeff, a KKK Imperial Wizard, comes onstage. Grand Dragon Mike reappears also. They are kept far from where Irv sits.

With fewer hoods and uniforms, the gang's all back.

Jerry wonders whether these groups can ever find coexistence. Mike says yes, **"As long as he admits that he's inferior to me."** Irv says that **"Never again will we back down from bullies."** This veiled Holocaust reference prompts a lecture from Jerry: **"Having suffered the exact same experience that you did, losing my family in the Holocaust, what I would say the lesson of that is never, ever, again do we judge human beings based on what they are instead of what they do."** The audience roars in agreement.

But this panel clearly is not ready for such brotherly love.

Jeff: **Why do you have the thought that we hate blacks? We hate niggers. They come in all colors, like that Jew bastard said.**

Mike (to Irv): **You got a disease. It's for you monetary capitalistic gain and the way you conduct business, Jew-boy.**

Irv: **My people can make more money by accident than you can ever make on purpose. And that's why you hate us.**

The Klan crew scream profanities in unison at Irv, who chants back, **"Trailer trash, trailer trash!"** Jeff heads over to pick a fight, but the security men jump in. Finally, a black man in the audience tells Mike that if his group is indeed not about hate but about doing good as they keep insisting, why not come to his Detroit neighborhood and let him and his buddies sign up. It's a wonderful idea in an ideal world, but one bigoted Mike can't possibly entertain: **"I've been to Detroit. You burn your own beautiful buildings down, Negro,"** he responds.

What's It All About, Jerry?

"Though they can be dismissed for being loony, their message, if ignored, can too easily become a growing cancer in our society. And it's not as if this hasn't happened before. If there's a lesson in all of this today, it's that we may all be offended by how they look, but what is really scary and dangerous are their ideas.

"Till next time, take care of yourself and each other."

"Wait a minute, I've just been demoted! Tonia said that, being Jewish, I was running the world and now you say I'm a slave!"

Woman in Labor Confronts Mistress

Two-timing men are nothing new, at least not on the *Jerry Springer Show*, but this episode offers prime examples of two shameless double-timers: men involved with two women simultaneously, who see no need to pick just one person. Oh, and in each relationship, one of the women is pregnant.

The first and most dramatic example, Nancy, is eight months pregnant—and currently in labor! She had wanted to confront the other woman before the baby was born and get her man to choose. But on the morning of the taping she unexpectedly went into labor and was rushed to the hospital. Incredibly, she checked herself out of the hospital and demanded to appear at the taping. So here she is—with contractions three minutes apart, paramedics checking her at every commercial break, and a very nervous Jerry checking on her condition.

Aired October 30, 1997

"You're having contractions right now! You're not going to have a baby here?!"

Madonna To Be

To wild applause, Nancy appears in her hospital gown covered by an oversized bathrobe bearing a "JS" monogram. Her hospital ID bracelet is quite evident, and Jerry is quite unnerved. **"If you think you are having the child, we'll stop the show. I want no surprises."** When Nancy indicates the contractions are already 3 minutes apart and she is dilated 4 centimeters, Jerry looks shaken. **"Are you trying to scare me?"**

Nancy and her boyfriend Versell live together, and already have a 1-year-old. Yet for the past three months this man has taken up with another girlfriend, Tara. **"This other woman is a bitch, she's a whore. She needs to stay the hell away from my man and find her own."**

She's here, she's in labor, get used to it.

Quite a Different Story

Tara comes out and heads right for Nancy, calling her the whore. She says that Nancy's the one who sleeps around, that she even recently went to North Carolina to be with a man. She claims that Versell is only staying with Nancy until paternity tests reveal if he is the true father. Moreover, she says that Nancy has tacitly approved of their affair.

Tara: **He slept with me two days ago.**
Nancy: **That's what she says.**
Tara: **Nancy, you babysitted the kids while we went out. And we slept in your bed. You said you knew that because you found one of my cigarettes in your bed.**
Nancy: **I didn't know you all was sleeping. I thought y'all was friends. That's all I thought.**

Still nervous about Nancy's condition, Jerry instructs the two women to separate their chairs, and **"please, no hitting!"**

It's going to take more than a contraction to scare Tara off.

"If you're gonna be with me ya'll gotta get along."

This Is Him?

As soon as the audience sees Versell they go nuts. Versell is a strikingly large, brown-skinned man with long black hair pulled into a pony tail. He wears a completely black suit accented by a silver necklace. He admits he started **"messing around with Tara"** after Nancy got pregnant, and claims he's not sure he's the father.

Backstage Secrets—Revealed!

The night before this show was taped, Nancy called producer Gina Huerta to announce that, though she was not due for another month, she was now in labor. (Apparently, her boyfriend Versell had been with his mistress Tara that night, and Nancy went out searching for them. A fight ensued, and then Versell returned to the hotel with Nancy—where they had sex. The whole escapade triggered her contractions.)

Gina decided to scratch their segment from the program. An hour before the taping, Gina called to check on Nancy's condition; she panicked when Nancy wasn't in her room. A few minutes later Nancy walked into the studio, still in her hospital gown, slippers, and wristband ID. She had checked out against her doctor's advice, and insisted on confronting her man's mistress. The producers agreed to let Nancy tell her story, as long as she agreed that a team of paramedics could stand by.

Paramedics truly are standing by.

Lynn is pregnant, too.

But Robyn doesn't care.

Though Jerry is a nervous wreck, Versell is an oasis of peace, unconcerned about Nancy's physical situation or the battle between his women. Unbelievably full of himself, Versell's position is that, **"They both can't leave me."**

Tough gal Nancy assumes her street-fighting stance as she recounts an incident from the other day. **"Tara said she was gonna have sex with Versell in my face, and I said, 'I'll be damned if she's gonna do that,' and I grabbed her hair and I hit her with the phone. I'm from New York, and I don't take no [bleep] from nobody!"** Then Nancy turns her wrath on Versell: **"If you were such a pimp daddy, you would be rich right now, but you're so broke people got to buy you [bleep]."**

Jerry can't imagine why either of the women would want to be with such a man, but each still demands that Versell choose.
Versell: **My decision is I'm gonna keep both of y'all.** (He plans on being by Nancy's side at the hospital, but he also plans on bringing Tara with him.)
Nancy: **You can't do that. You'll end up get-**

ting killed. You won't have that pretty hair no more.
Versell: **If I can't have my women together, I don't want them at all.**

Both women refuse to be part of his harem, but he insists **"it will happen. I'm gonna put them together."**

Knocked Up

At least Lynn is only two months pregnant, but she and Jason have been married for four years and have a 3-year-old child. Lynn is here to tell her husband's mistress to butt out.
Lynn: **She don't know how to keep her legs closed. She goes for anybody that's married. Y'all got to watch your men.**
Jerry: **Well, we have security here in the audience.**

Mistress Robyn emerges to dispute Lynn's claim that she is the one pursuing Jason.
Robyn: **If he's happy, then why is he knocking on my door every night?**
Lynn: **He ain't knocking on your [bleep] door because you're out [bleep]ing everybody else!**

Lynn stands and challenges Robyn to "kick my ass." An agitated Jerry shouts, "No! Not while you're pregnant!" Whoever's at fault, it's clear that Jason is two-timing both women. He had sex with Robyn three days ago, and was intimate with his wife just last night.

Update!

After Nancy gave birth she came back for a show update. The producers expected that Nancy would have left Versell. They were shocked to discover that not only hadn't Nancy left Versell, but they were married. And he was still seeing his mistress, Tara.

Lynn demonstrates the traditional position of Robyn's legs.

Jason tells his "violent" wife he wants out.

And Knocked Out

Husband Jason emerges in a purple suit, arms raised in victory, to the same boos that greeted Robyn. He goes straight to Robyn and kisses her; Lynn stands, takes off her wedding ring and throws it at Jason. Robyn smiles victoriously—until Lynn smacks her across her face. **"She ain't nothing but a whore. I gave you four good years!"** she cries to her husband.

Even Jerry can't believe that Jason would humiliate his wife on national TV, however much he might love Robyn. But Jason says the marriage has not been the joy that Lynn has claimed. Lynn has uncontrollable, violent anger; she even threw a brick at someone's window. He says she has called the cops on him. Jason says he has long asked Lynn for a divorce and desperately wants one so he can be with Robyn, but she refuses. Once when he tried to leave the house, **"she forced me to stay inside."** He sounds like a guy who genuinely wants out of his marriage, and yet he has no good answers for why he doesn't just leave—and why he keeps sleeping with his wife if the marriage is over.

What's It All About, Jerry?

"If you are being cheated on, or shared, and you know about it, then it is purely your decision as to whether you want to continue in this often painful situation. We may grow to hate what a lover does to us when he or she beds down with another, but the truth is, we inevitably get treated the way we allow ourselves to be treated. It hurts to leave a lover, but if a lover cheats, he or she has already left.

"Till next time, take care of yourself and each other."

"Just don't name this kid Jerry Springer."

I'm Pregnant by a Transsexual

e've seen transsexuals. We've seen fights. We've seen irate viewers. And we've seen repeat guests. But here we have the audience's favorite transsexual Brittany, soon to be a father, taking on two viewers in a brawl that never ends. Of course along the way there are dilemmas (will Brittany be the mother or the father?), divas (Brittany's mom is a force of nature), and disclosures (the mother-to-be's sister doesn't know Brittany is the father-to-be)—though these are mere opening acts for the battle royale.

Aired November 3, 1997

"Is your child going to call you mom or dad?"

"She's" Back!

When last we met gender-challenged Brittany, "she" was breaking the news about her transsexuality to fiancé David (see, "My Girlfriend's a Guy"), and announcing her engagement to Rodney.

But all the dudes are ditched and Brittany is **"deeply in love now. This person accepts me for who I am."** This person is Dee, a self-professed ladies' woman, who knows all about Brittany's true identity. And Dee reveals, she is 4 months pregnant—with Brittany's child! Jerry is flummoxed. He wonders whether Brittany is ready for the responsibility of, uh, fatherhood: **"When your kid comes home from school, are you going to be wearing the dress?"** Brittany admits this recent turn of events has him confused. First he says yes, but then confesses that he just doesn't know.

Sisterly Advice

Brittany's sister Braetta is here to say, **"Brittany, it's time to hang up the dress, take the shoes off, and be a father to your child!"** Apparently, Brittany has another child, but one the child's mother doesn't let Brittany see. As Braetta puts it, **"He doesn't see the child because he's wearing a [bleep] dress."**

The Lesbians Circle the Wagons

Dee's two friends, June and Wheeze, appear next. Apparently they provide a cushy shoulder for Dee when she and Brittany have **"altercations,"** as Brittany puts it. June is a bit more blunt: **"Dee don't need to be with Brittany because Brittany is whipping Dee's ass."**

But it seems they may have an ulterior motive in splitting Dee from Brittany—keeping her in the lesbian fold.

Wheeze: **Dee, you got to get rid of Brittany. Straight up. I mean, I thought you was gay.**

Brittany: **They are just jealous, because they want some [bleep] too.**

Mom's In Charge Now

Brittany's mom Vera comes out looking cross. Brittany tries to kiss her but she pulls away. Vera looks him in the eye and sternly declares: **"Y'all need to get it together. The baby's not gonna have two mamas. It's only going to have a mother and a father."**

Vera's got some angry words for Dee, also: **"You need to keep your business and your laundry at home, between you and Brittany."**

But it seems that Vera has a tender heart. She lovingly accepted her son's unconventional life choice many years ago. **"I'm gonna love him if he be a woman or a man."**

Dee and Brittany are having a baby.

Dee's lesbian pals don't approve.

Brittany's mom says it's time to be man.

Dee's sister Wanda had no idea.

Life in the Ring

Brittany and the other transsexuals who appear on *Springer* prove to be one of the biggest challenges for Steve Wilkos and his security staff. **"You try to deal with women differently than men,"** Steve explains. **"A man you can just bullrush, but a woman you try to handle in a more gentle way."** So how to handle a transsexual? It's mind-bending, Steve says, because **"you're looking at a woman, and then she turns around and slugs you with a lot of force!"** Worse, in tackling this show, Steve was one security guy short of his usual five.

The women taunting Brittany proved to be a handful as well. As stage manager Todd Schultz admits, **"Those women were really tough. No matter what I did, they kept getting away from me."**

A Shocker for Sis

Brittany may have an understanding family, but that doesn't seem to be the case for Dee. Her sister Wanda apparently hasn't a clue even that her sister is a lesbian. Dee quickly reveals, **"You thought Brittany was my best friend. Brittany is my lover."** The sister looks pained, as if she might soon need a stretcher, but Dee's confession has only just begun: **"She's also my baby's father."** A stunned Wanda covers her face. Tears stream down her face, and her hands shake as she tries to wipe them away.

Jerry gives Wanda a tissue and tries to be sympathetic. No doubt mom Vera thinks she's helping, too, when she says to Wanda: **"I would like to welcome you to our family, because Dee is already welcomed."** Wanda might as well accept this circus as reality, Vera tells her, because **"there's nothing none of us can**

You'll Never Marry My Brother!

elissa could surely qualify as one of the world's most overprotective big sisters, and she will stop at almost nothing to keep her brother Damian from marrying "that slut" Mary. That includes beating up Mary repeatedly. As always, the full picture and the final results are more than we would have imagined: Damien's temper, Mary's temptations, two tempestuous friends, and a surprise ending await.

Aired November 4, 1997

"Let's get through five minutes without hitting here."

In this corner, Mary: pound for pound one of the scrappiest *Springer* guests ever.

Does this look like a fair match-up?

How could anyone stand in the way of true love?

Let the Games Begin!

Exchange that provokes catfight #1: Melissa has several good reasons why her 19-year-old brother shouldn't marry 17-year-old Mary, including, **"she cheats on my brother, she lies to my brother, and she manipulates my brother."**

Exchange that provokes catfight #2: Mary gives a less-than-sterling denial that she cheats. Mary (in a thick, southern drawl: **I've left him for one time—or twice—and she knows that.** Melissa: **What do you do at your mother's when you say you want to go up there?** Mary: **I go up to my best friend.** Melissa: **You're such a liar!** The women jump up and push each other; Jerry intervenes: **"There will be no close dancing!"**

Exchange that provokes catfight #3: It seems Mary lives with Melissa and Damian's family. Melissa: **When are you going to get a job and get out of my mother's house?** Mary: **I am not the one who wanted to move in there. He's the one that wanted you to watch over me. Which I don't need a [bleep] babysitter.**

Exchange that almost provokes catfight #4:
Mary: **I've only left him once, uh, twice.**
Melissa: **That's enough.**
Mary: **Because he hit me.**
Melissa: **He pushed you.**
Mary: **Then why did your husband have to pull him off of me?**
Melissa: **Because you threw a lighter on him! A hot Zippo lighter.**

Mary: **That's [bleep]. I was turning around. He had already slapped me.**
Melissa: **I'd have slapped your ass, too!**

It is soon revealed that Mary was married once before. This year. For a month.

The Object of Their Aggression

As Damian enters, Mary rises—not to fight, but to kiss Damian. He pulls away, demanding to know if Mary is cheating. She says she is not. Melissa offers her own helpful advice: **"I love you, Damian, but I don't know why your self-esteem is so low that you've got to chase this little slut right here"** (a statement that, not surprisingly, provokes catfight #5).

Melissa brings up a guy named Scott, **"the last little victim Mary got."** It seems that during the one, uh, two times that Mary left Damian, she landed in Scott's arms. **"Butt out, bitch,"** Mary commands. And it seems Scott is here today.

The Dogfight

Scott appears bearing a bouquet of roses, which he hands to Mary. Damian asks: **"If she loves me, wouldn't she throw them roses on the floor?"** Mary gives them back to Scott and kisses Damian.

Winning his woman is apparently not enough for Damian. He goads Scott, **"I slapped you like a little bitch,**

Laugh of the Show

Jerry to Mary: **"You were married a month! Did the divorce take longer than the marriage?**

101

Sometimes it's more fun to fight in front of your man.

Sometimes he wants to get in on the action, too.

Scott has no idea what will really happen to those flowers.

didn't I, little bitch?" Soon, the flowers are back in Mary's hands. Damian grabs the bouquet and starts beating Scott with it.

The bottom line, as we learn, is that Mary and Scott didn't have sex, but they did mess around. Mary values Scott for listening to her, and not hitting her, but Damian is the one she loves. Melissa resolutely insists that her brother is not violent, though it's apparent to all of us that he has a hot temper. Even he admits that he has a problem.

The Avenger

From here the parade of friends gets more confusing. Buck seems to be a former friend of Damian's and a current friend of Mary's, and he's angry that Damian is picking on defenseless people. **"You want to hit a woman? You want to hit a little guy?"** he screams, heading for Damian. Buck pulls Damian's hair as the men wrestle each other to the ground. Sensing the opportunity, the women go after each other, too. Jerry is pleased when security separates everyone's chairs. He jokes: **"We spend all this money on furniture, and they...."**

Update!

True to his desire, Jerry did soon have Damian and Mary return to the show. The update segment proved that sister knows best, because the unhappy honeymooners were no longer together. Mary was now sleeping with Damian's good friend, while Damian had a new squeeze of his own.

In the first sensible advice of the program—which elicits cheers from the audience—Buck says that hitting a woman is never an answer.

Buck: **He threw Mary into the entertainment center.**

Damian: **I didn't throw her through no entertainment center. I pushed her into it.**

Melissa—ever-faithful in defending her brother—is now mad at Buck for pulling Damian's hair. **"That was chicken [bleep] to pull his hair. Girls pull hair!"**

Bloody Marys

Another, larger Mary angrily joins the panel and shoves Mary #1, who challenges her right back. Jerry offers her some advice: "You're 96 pounds. It's not productive to say to people, 'Come on, let's fight.'"

The women trade charges that each is a "bitch." It seems that both Marys worked together, and for reasons that never become clear, Mary #2 is also very upset about this planned wedding and wants to stop it.

Down on One Knee

Damian takes his Mary aside and goes down on one knee (the only time he's been on the floor by his own choosing!).

Buck: **That's another one of them Kmart rings?**

Mary #2: **That's all the bitch is worth.... Damian, I'm not going to [bleep] let a friend marry a bitch like that.**

Damian greets Buck the same way he greeted Scott.

Mary vs. Mary: "Bitch!" "I'm a better bitch than you."

Till death do us part—or till February?

Mary #1: **And what do you think you are?**
Mary #2: **I'm a better bitch than you** (they assume catfight position).

Damian wants to know if Mary will marry him here and now. She agrees. Will Buck be the best man? Buck's return gesture—likely involving his tallest finger—is made visually incomprehensible by the censors. He cautions Mary: **"If he beats you once, he'll beat you twice."**

Wedded Bliss?

During the commercial break, Mary slips into a bridal gown while Damian dons a tux. Jerry introduces the Reverend Peter Flessas, **"a gentleman who is with us on many of these ceremonies that we have on our show here."**

Damian lovingly watches Mary walk through the audience. They exchange vows, but Damian doesn't have another ring. The Reverend is nonplussed: **"All right, if you don't have it, we don't need it."** He pronounces them man and wife.

Melissa's one hope is that her brother **"has $500 for a divorce in a month."** Mary #2 offers: **"I wish she'd burn in hell."** (Jerry points out that this is a harsh sentiment for a newlywed.)

Jerry invites the newly united pair to come back on the show in a year, **"hopefully as a married couple, and you will have proven most of us wrong,"** or as singletons, and **"we'll find out why it didn't work out."**

What's It All About, Jerry?

"Rare is the case when someone 17, 18, or 19 has the maturity, wisdom, experience and sense of perspective usually necessary to give a marriage any realistic sense of surviving. Even if they do love each other, love is a reason to want to be married, it is never a reason by itself to be married. I'm not saying these two can't ever make it, but there's an awful lot of work that needs to be done if a marriage here is to be anything more than a long and difficult date.

"Till next time, take care of yourself and each other."

Backstage Secrets—Revealed!

Studio weddings have become such a staple of the show that the women's wardrobe closet features rows of white satin pumps. The producers can also supply a dress, a tux, flowers, cake, and even a small cubic zirconia engagement ring. (A whole stash of such rings is always on hand.)

Of course *Springer* weddings have their challenges. In a different episode, the cake actually became a hazard when a guest heaved the fifteen-pound creation. Steve Wilkos recalls seeing the cake bulleting towards his face, and ducking just in time. A fellow security guard, Jimmy Sherlock, wasn't so lucky. The huge chocolate cake hit his head dead on. Looking like a chocolate creature from the black lagoon with two white eyes peeking out, Jimmy was so thoroughly covered that he couldn't wash it all off that afternoon; he picked cake out of his ears for days afterward.

Lovers vs. Mistresses

*T*he women in this show came here to battle their mistresses—and battle they do! One woman goes after her husband's lover on 10 separate occasions. Lisa heaps so much abuse on Sara that even Jerry gets tuckered out—from watching! But she finally uses her brain instead of her fists to ask herself the question we in the audience have wondered all along: Why is she going to blows for a man who is two-timing her? It's a query the lovers in the other two segments should be pondering for themselves, also.

Aired April 17, 1998

By the Numbers

1 (guy-guy battles)

3 (guy-gal battles)

13 (gal-gal battles)

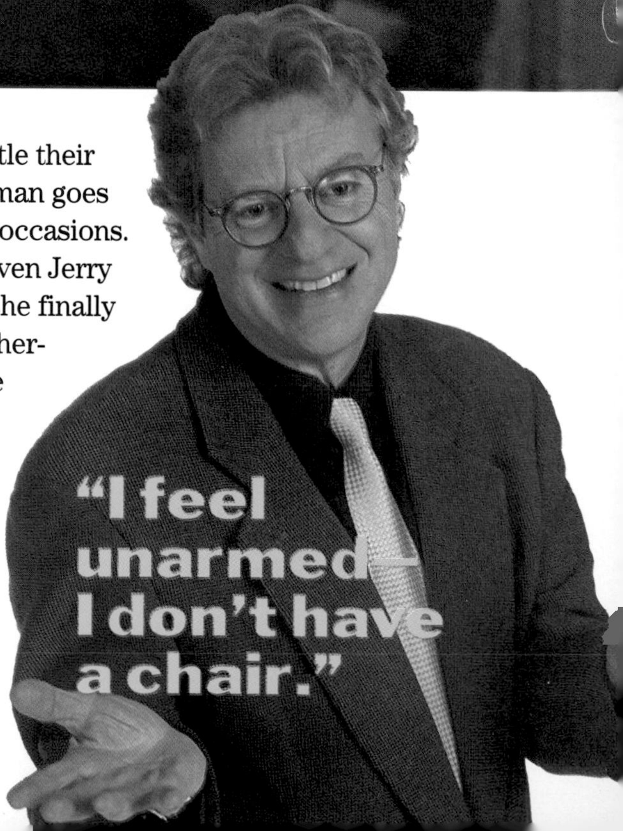

"I feel unarmed— I don't have a chair."

A Friend, Indeed!

Lisa is fighting mad that her lover's old girlfriend is still trying to win him away. **"The bitch just won't leave me or my boy alone. She follows us around, she sends him Valentine's cards. I'm sick of her."** Lisa is apparently handling this problem the mature way: **"I've done been to jail for beatin' this bitch's ass."** She admits that Sara actually dated Gwain first, but says she and her man have been living together for the past two years, and share a child.

As Sara comes out she is met at the entrance by Lisa, who attacks her right off. Sara savagely fights back. When they finally calm down Jerry gets to the story. Sara and Lisa were once best friends, and Sara even let her pal move in with her and her boyfriend, Gwain. Then, **"I came home from work and they were screwing in my bed!"** Sara says Gwain keeps coming to her, not the other way around. They slept together as recently as two weeks ago, **"and it was good, too, bitch!"** Lisa claims her lover will deny that, and that **"he ain't gonna lie to me."** Jerry sarcastically asks: **"Why would a guy ever lie?"** But should it prove to be true? Lisa says, **"I'll beat the hell out of him!"**

But first she's not through doing the same to Sara. They tangle another seven times during this segment—pulling hair, leaping through the air to jump on each other, and more. Once Lisa even picks up her chair to heave at Sara (ably blocked by quick-acting stage manager, Todd Schultz), prompting Jerry to remark: **"I feel unarmed. I don't have a chair!"**

The Man in the Middle

Gwain sits between the women and reaches for Lisa's hand. **"We're tight. Me and Lisa are tight."** But Gwain soon admits that he also **"cares for Sara,"** and that he is still having sex with her. Lisa springs up, livid: **"You are?"** She slaps Gwain's face. Sara uses this distraction to leap over for her own shot at Lisa, and the women fight again. Lisa tells her man they're through: **"I'm gonna get me somebody else."**

Sara's brother Jack comes out to avenge her honor. **"You can do ten times better than Bubba Gump right here,"** Jack says. He heads for Gwain and another brawl ensues. The men hold each other in a head lock, pirouetting around the stage and knocking chairs to the floor. When the security guys sit Gwain down, Jack heads for Lisa again.
Jack: **I'm tired of him playing my sister like she's some kind of ho or something!**
Gwain and Lisa in unison: **She is!**

The Lovers

Lisa's already "been to jail for beating this bitch's ass."

Angelina's here to take on what she describes as a clothes-stealing, man-poaching, bitch.

Deborah suspects her lesbian lover has been cheating.

Unanswered Questions:

Was it Sara or Gwain who initiated their recent fling?

Did Karnell ever sleep with Starla? It certainly seems likely.

Who *does* have Kristy's underwear?

Shontae is the natural mother of her and Deborah's baby, but how did they manage the father's part?

If Deborah is involved with a guy now, why is she even on the show fighting for Shontae?

Sara tells Lisa that he's *my* man.

Starla says he came looking for *her*.

She's not feisty, she's Heaven.

So who does Gwain choose? He shocks everyone: **"I ain't wild about neither one of them."** Lisa realizes that her heroic battle has been for naught. **"I can't believe I'm fighting over your damn sorry non-working [bleep, bleep] ass!"**

The War of the Women, Part Two

Next up is Angelina, who says she is fed up with another woman, Starla, meddling in her marriage. **"This bitch came into my house, tried to sleep with my man, she's going around saying she's pregnant by him even though she never slept with him. She stole my husband's clothes, my baby's clothes. She's so nasty she stole my sister-in-law's underwear!"** Starla met Angelina's husband Karnell at a bar. **"She's a bar junkie,"** she says condescendingly. **"And your husband was just there delivering pizza?"** Jerry wonders.

As Starla comes onstage, Angelina goes to ambush her, but the pair somehow end up on opposite sides of the chairs. They pause for a moment to ponder the barricade, but decide they're not about to let some chairs stop them. They fight right over the chairs.

Angelina: **I thought my husband had better taste!**

Starla: **Bitch, let me tell you something. Your man came to me. Evidently you ain't no good for him to come to me.**

Don't Cry for Me, Angelina

Karnell comes out and kisses his wife. He admits that he **"fooled around"** with Starla while he and Angelina were separated, but denies that they slept together. Jerry clarifies: **"In other words, you were awake the whole time."**

Karnell easily chooses his wife, but Starla doesn't seem to mind: **"I think I can do a lot better than this [bleep] here."** This prompts Angelina to rise and pounce once more on her adversary. They pull each other's hair. When Karnell tries to

Take that, you man-stealing ex-friend.

Angelina came to tangle, but Starla's got her hair in knots.

Deborah (left) is the only lover who stays in her chair.

106

reign his wife in, she turns on him, yelling, **"Don't protect that! What I came out here to do was to kick her ass!"**

Angelina has a final message for Starla from her sister-in-law, the one who is minus a few key pieces of clothing: **"Kristy says she wants her boots and her underwears back."**

Getting to Heaven

The final love triangle features Deborah, who says she and her lover have been together for 2½ years and share a daughter. They had planned several wedding dates—Valentine's Day, her birthday, New Year's Eve, **"and a double wedding with my mama"**—but all came and went. Lately, things haven't been going right. **"I just want to know where I stand, where we're going to go from here."**

Her lover comes out to a startled audience, because she is a woman. Lover Shontae quickly admits, **"I've been seeing somebody else."** And out comes a hot bleached-blond in a too-tight silver dress named Heaven. The women engage in a long sensuous kiss while the audience shrieks. Heaven is tired of Shontae's playing the field and wants her to commit.

Shontae admits that she has also lied to Heaven, but that **"I'm trying to come clean with my lies, and I'm being faithful to you right now. You are who I want to be with."** Quips Jerry: **"She's trying to get to Heaven."**

That proves fine with Deborah, who confesses she has moved on already: **"I'm in love with a man now."**

What's It All About, Jerry?

"In romantic terms, we're not capable of loving more than one, because love means giving all of yourself to someone. If you're splitting your affection, then neither lover is getting anything you hold special. So you do have to choose. A great lover is measured not by the quantity of his lovers. In love, the only number is one.

"Till next time, take care of yourself and each other."

The Kisses

Gwain reaches out to Lisa (but he later admits reaching out to Sara, too).

Karnell kisses Angelina (but later he defends Starla from Angelina).

Shontae kisses Heaven (but later says she's not ready to be with just one person).

Wives Battle Mistresses!

he producers were serious when they put "battle" in the title of this episode. This show features four fighting females who are as "hot out of the box" as *Springer* guests get. Vicky is so pissed at her husband's mistress she's willing to risk everything, including her hairdo. But this soon turns out to be no more than a warm-up bout for the second round.

Aired April 27, 1998

The Opening Bell

Vicki presents herself as the victim, but as we know, on this show there are always at least three sides to every story. Vicki and Jason have been married for four years and share three children, but his mistress Lisa keeps getting in the way. **"This bitch is interfering into our lives. I'm sick of it. I'm just gonna hurt her when she gets out here."** Jerry pleads for restraint, but there's no appeasing Vicki. **"I've whupped her ass one time"** already. Of course, she's also furious at her disloyal husband. **"I've whupped his ass one time before, and I'm gonna whip it again."**

Vicki is a strong woman, with one of the foulest mouths in TV-land. Throughout the show she wrestles control of the show from Jerry. She doesn't care that Jerry wants to ask questions. **"Screw it. I'm ready. Let's bring her out."**

The Challenger

Lisa comes onstage and runs straight for Vicki. The gals jump on each other. Knocked off balance, they land in a heap on the floor, but they don't lose a beat, continuing to go at it as the crowd cheers. When the security guys finally upright them, Vicki's still got a grip on Lisa's long hair. It takes three men to finally set Lisa free. Even then, Vicki gets one last shot in before taking her seat.

Jerry waits patiently while the women button their shirts and adjust their bra straps. He finally asks: **"Have you two met?"**

This turns out to be the only question he can ask for some time. He tries to get Lisa's side of the story, but Vicki constantly interrupts with her name-calling. Jerry is frustrated that he can't get a word in.

Jerry (to Vicki): **Let her answer.**

Vicki: **No.**

Jerry (jumping up and down like a child): **Hey, hey—it's my show!**

But today it's clearly The Vicki Show. After she tries a second run at Lisa, she's ready to take on philandering Jason.

Vicki: **Bring him out, bring him out!**

Jerry: **Next segment.**

Vicki: **I don't care. Bring him out now!**

Finally, Jerry gets to ask a question, and it's a good one. When did each woman last have sex with Jason?

Lisa: **Monday night.**

Vicki: **Monday night.**

Jerry (eyes opening wide): **How busy *is* this guy?**

It's Vicki, the Marital Magician: she slices, she dices, she shreds clothing—and she whups ass.

But, says Jason, she doesn't cook or clean or give him sex.

Jason Takes His Lickin'

The crowd boos as a nervous-looking Jason enters. He justifies his affair with Lisa: **"Vicki don't act like my wife anymore."** Vicki stands and screams at him, **"I don't? I don't?"** Jason answers that **"the only time you clean up the house, cook, or even give me sex is when you find out I have somebody else."**

Vicki pulls out a blue man's shirt from under her chair, apparently a gift from Lisa to Jason. As she says she has done with other such offerings, Vicki tears the shirt apart.

Mistress Lisa comes onstage with a running start.

The Ambush

Vicki's friend Bridget comes out and stands in front of Jason's chair. She shakes her left hand at Jason, chastising him for his behavior—but then she goes after a surprised Lisa with her right hand. Soon thereafter, she moves on to Jason. (He later claims, to great dispute, that he slept with Bridget in 1992.)

When things finally get civilized, Jerry asks Jason to choose his woman. He turns to Lisa and takes her hand. **"My wife and I are not going to be together."** Always needing to get the last word in, Vicki shouts back, **"There's better out there than you! You can keep this little [bleep] trash!"** But her heart still longs for Jason, and she is sure he secretly feels the same way.

Friend Bridget comes onstage with a surprise greeting.

In a rare moment, Misty is both seated and not cursing.

As promised, Misty tries to kick Anna out of her life.

Mr. Innocent?

"He's saying that now because he's in front of y'all, but when he gets home it's going to be a totally different story. He's going to be there with me, so I'm not even worried."

Don't Play Misty!

We may have thought Vicki was strong-willed, but that's because we hadn't met the next angry wife, Misty. Misty's here to take on her husband Jeremy's mistress, Anna, a woman with whom Jeremy recently had a child. It seems that Misty and her hubby had a little fight, and he ended up in Anna's arms: "She spread her legs as wide as she could and he stuck [bleep] and got her pregnant." Misty and Jeremy (who have their own baby) are divorcing, but she says they will still live together. "It's going to be a lot different this time. Everyone's going to play by *my* rules." The idea seems to be that she will keep him close by so that she can torture him.

Bring It On

Anna comes out yelling a string of censored epithets. As with the earlier fight, these women also mean business. They jump each other and land on the ground, in the spot warmed up earlier by Vicki and Lisa. Legs fly in all directions. Suddenly, an unidentified woman is also on them! (We'll later discover it's Anna's friend Melissa.) The security men quickly remove the gal, then turn their attention to Misty, who has a hold on Anna's short hair.

They are finally separated, but Misty isn't through. "Do you want some more?" she taunts. And more she gets. Even then Misty doesn't let her prey rest: "Cry honey, cry. Come on. I see that mascara smearing."

After the break we learn that Anna is also married. So why is she involved with Misty's man? "She likes getting kicked to the curb, I think," Misty answers. And Misty clearly relishes doing it.

The Weak Link

Jeremy enters and sits by his soon-to-be-ex, Misty. She immediately looks him up and down and announces her displeasure with his outfit: "I don't like that. You need to change." Jeremy seems to enjoy being pussy-whipped. Instead of walking away he declares, "I love Misty, with all my heart." Later he tells the audience he's proud of her strong ways.

Anna is visibly upset. "It's lame that you took me to your wife's house to [bleep]

Anna claims that, "He likes these."

But Jeremy portrays his vision of them.

me." She tells him she loves him, **"and you know for a fact I would do anything for you."** Jeremy is skeptical: **"You really love me? You got married a month after we split up."**

The Mystery Fighter

Now we officially meet Anna's friend Melissa, the woman who unexpectedly jumped into the earlier fight. As she enters, Misty stands up and kicks away her chair to make room for this next tangle. The women brawl again, with Melissa pulling on Misty's hair, and Misty grabbing at Melissa's shirt so hard she nearly rips it off (she doesn't, but we do see plenty of Melissa's jiggling belly!). Ever the street fighter, Misty keeps goading her even after the battle is over: **"Come on, you want some more?"** As she finally calms down she casually observes, **"Oh, I've got cotton mouth again."**

So why did Anna think that Jeremy would prefer her? **"I am more woman than this little girl will ever be."** Anyway, Anna's got another ace up her sleeve—or rather, her shirt. **"He likes these,"** she says, lifting her red top to reveal large breasts in a black bra. Most in the audience cheer the move, although at least one woman covers her man's eyes. Jeremy laughs. **"She's a slut,"** he declares. A woman in the audience corrects him: **"No, you're the slut. And the ones that are paying are all the kids."**

What's It All About, Jerry?

So many *Springer* shows deal with scorned wives confronting their husband's mistresses, that Jerry occasionally reaches into his storehouse of classic conclusions for an apt "Final Thought." This one comes from "Woman in Labor Confronts Mistress":

"If you are being cheated on, or shared, and you know about it, then it is purely your decision as to whether you want to continue in this often painful situation. We may grow to hate what a lover does to us when he or she beds down with another, but the truth is, we inevitably get treated the way we allow ourselves to be treated. It hurts to leave a lover, but if a lover cheats, he or she has already left.

"Till next time, take care of yourself and each other."

"You two are fighting over this guy that sleeps with both of you!"

Ex-Lovers Confronted!

hris is tired of having her boyfriend's old girlfriend, Joy, hound her man. She's ready to confront Joy—and Joy, who seems to live in a fantasy world, is equally up for the encounter. Security chief Steve Wilkos earns his stripes in this episode, as he furiously works to keep Joy and her brazen friend Diane from treating Chris like a human punching bag. It turns out to be a small price for Chris to pay, because, although she loses the battle she certainly wins the war: Shawn gets down on one knee and pops the question onstage. (Of course, even this romantic moment is interrupted by Joy). Later in the show another two women hankering after the same guy also get into a tussle, causing one woman to pull the other's wig right off her head.

Aired April 30, 1998

By the Numbers

11 (number of times Chris tangles with an adversary)

2 (seconds it seems Joy can stay in a chair)

1 (number of women onstage happy with the behavior of their man)

Who's the "Slut"?

Chris says she and her man Shawn are trying to have a nice quiet relationship, but they are stalked, harassed, and paged to death by Shawn's old flame, Joy. **"She calls us all the time, she drives by his work, she shows up at our house, she threatens my son."** They even tried moving to a new home, but Joy found them. Chris says she and her beau have been together for three years, and that she won him fair and square. **"I did not steal him; he was out looking for somebody else because she's a bitch."**

Out storms a very joyless Joy. The women trade inaudible epithets until Jerry calms them enough to get a so-called dialogue going:

Joy: **He's not my *ex*-boyfriend. We've been together for the last four years.**

Chris: **No you haven't. He's been living with me for three years. He sleeps with me every night....**

Joy: **Shut up, you little slut.**

Chris: **No. You're the slut.**

Joy claims she has had sex often with Shawn and even recently got pregnant but miscarried, facts which Shawn later vehemently denies. Joy is sure she is a better catch than Chris, even if Shawn can't see it: **"She can't get a man because she's too damn ugly. She's nothing but a [bleep]. Now *this* is a woman** (Joy stands and struts her own stuff). **These are boobs!"**

The First Punch. And the Second...

Shawn enters to jeers and he responds with pirouettes; clearly he thinks he's worth fighting over! Shawn claims that Joy is living in a fantasy world when she says they've recently been together. **"The last time was almost three years ago. I haven't slept with her since."**

The two women soon stand and challenge one another. Shawn tries to position himself between them, but they are determined to reach around him. Joy pushes Chris and knocks her off balance.

Soon Joy's friend Diane comes onstage to join the fray. She heads right for Chris. **"This little bitch right here does not deserve to be with him,"** The women's anger now turns to Shawn. Joy accuses him of being **"a deadbeat father."** With that, everyone is up, and Joy seeks out Chris yet again.

More bickering ensues about who's lying about what when Joy slaps Chris again, momentarily pulling her hair. Chris retaliates by grabbing Joy's curly tresses and not letting go—even as Steve and several assistant try to pry the locks from her furious fingers. **"You don't deserve to sit by him,"** Diane shouts at Chris, but when she responds, **"He's my man and he's coming home with me!,"** Diane is on her feet again, this time putting Chris's long blond hair into a wrestler's hold. How riotous it looks when all three women finally take their seats (for a second, anyway) wearing the messiest bedroom hair ever on TV. Seconds later Joy rises again, but Shawn has had enough. **"Sit your happy ass down,"** he commands.

Joy (left) and Chris are both fighting for Shawn.

And he seems to like it that way.

Joy brings in reinforcements—her friend Diane.

But Shawn doesn't like that.

Hey, I'm trying to propose here.

Latoya says, "Bring that fat, cross-eyed bitch out there."

An Indecent Proposal

Jerry asks Shawn to decide. It's no contest. He walks towards Chris's chair, kneels before her, and reaches into his pocket for a ring. But Joy won't let even this go unchallenged. She's up slapping Chris before the ring gets on her finger, and then Shawn. (After the proposal, Shawn jumps up raging about her never hitting him again—a reaction he curiously didn't have when Joy was after his woman.) Finally, the ring goes on, and Chris says yes. As Jerry congratulates them, Diane gets the last, uh, word in—by taking off her shoes and throwing them at her.

Fighting Over a Confessed Two-Timer

In the next segment we meet Latoya, a woman who wants her husband Jerome's longtime—and very public—mistress out of her life. She relishes the confrontation: **"That bitch is mine. Bring that fat, cross-eyed bitch out here!"**

Sandra comes out and immediately removes her shoes. Latoya reciprocates, throwing her jacket to the floor. After they calm themselves down, they switch from brawling to bickering—over everything from who should get the guy to which one has the fatter ass.

Then Sandra fondles the silver necklace around her neck as a warning to Latoya to stop messing with her. Apparently, this necklace was given to her by Jerome (like a wedding ring for

Woman in audience: "You women up there are making all women across the country look stupid!"

Sandra's ready for action.

And action there is—flying wigs and all.

Jerome faces off against Latoya, and prepares to blow her off.

mistresses?), and Latoya knows it. But she's too mad to worry. **"I don't care!"** she screams as she grabs for and breaks the chain.

The ensuing battle quickly gets ugly, in more ways than one. As Sondra gropes Latoya's face she knocks off Latoya's wig, revealing the ponytail beneath it! Most women in such a hairless state would run for cover, but not Latoya. In fact, when a security man hands her the wig she tosses it up in the air and watches as it drops to the floor.

The Man in the Middle—and Loving It

Jerome soon appears and the audience is none-too-happy with him. With a self-confident flair he twirls his blue derby and drops it on his chair. Standing, he confronts Latoya, presumably for messing with his treasured necklace, but it's hard to hear under the string of censored epithets. **"Both you girls is acting like bitches right now,"** he says, demanding that Latoya **"sit your ass down."** Jerome makes it clear he's not giving up his mistress, Sandra. Having her hairpiece pulled off may not have upset her, but having her husband diss her before the world boils Latoya's blood. She takes off her wedding ring and throws it at him. **"You can go home with her!"** she screams. And Jerome certainly will. **"I have to be with two women to make a ho. But now I got my ho,"** he says, pointing to Sandra.

The audience's firmly believes that Latoya should leave Jerome. But will she? A man asks her honestly: **"When the lights are down and the camera's off, are you going to take him back?"** Latoya quietly answers: **"Maybe so. Probably yes."**

What's It All About, Jerry?

"In matters of the heart there is often no matter in the mind. The heart rules. You think there's always a chance. But ultimately, if someone is trying to steal your lover away, there is only one person who can put a stop to it all: your partner. In most cases a relationship gets interfered with only because someone lets it.

"Till next time, take care of yourself and each other."

"If it's clear that he doesn't want to be with you, why would you want to be with him?"

I Married a Horse

t the opening Jerry tells us, "There's been all this controversy about all the fights—well today we have a love story." Actually three love stories—each one so controversial and outrageous that after taping it was deemed unsuitable for broadcast, the first and only time a *Springer* show has been unaired. As the show title indicates, the panel members are all zoophiles: one man is literally married to his horse, and the others are sexually involved with their dogs. The rest you'll have to read to believe.

You must remember this! | This kiss is not just a kiss. | Pixel; or is it Mrs. Pixel?

The Stud

Jerry introduces Mark as a man who **"has been with his wife for 10 years and married for 5."** At first, Mark sits alone onstage, but his other half soon appears; the audience howls with surprise when they realize his lover is a mare. Before Jerry can even get a word in, Pixel and Mark engage in a long—and shocking—tongue-kiss. Whoomp, there it is. (As we later learn, Mark has even written a book on his affair, *The Horse-Man: Obsessions of a Zoophile*.)

Jerry immediately voices his—and all viewers'—opinion. **"This is pretty sick, isn't it?"** But Mark denies he is mentally imbalanced. **"A psychologist described it to me as an unusual adjustment to a unique situation."** More passionate tongue-thrusting between the pair follows, prompting Jerry to, well, reign them in: **"No making out onstage."**

Mark says he first realized he was beastosexual when, as a horny teen he was grooming his friend's grandmother's filly. **"She lifted her tail up and there it was in all it's glory."** Jerry immediately sits down. **"I'm going to vomit."**

Regaining his composure, Jerry asks the hard questions. Mark claims he had his first sexual encounter **"after a bad prom date."** Screwing the mare **"was great, fantastic."** Although he married a woman (later divorced for unrelated reasons) and fathered two kids, he never lost his thing for the fillies. He even cheated with horses while still married. Was his wife disgusted by his action? **"Well, I actually never asked her."**

What do his kids think? **"My daughter put it this way, 'You just march to the beat of a differ-ent hoof.'"** Jerry is revolted. **"Please don't tell me your kids say, 'Hey, Dad, if that's what you like, go to the derby. Really get turned on.'"**

Jerry stands up for the animal's rights:
Jerry: **Why do you think the horse is consenting to you getting on it and doing what you do to it?**
Mark: **One time I tried to force myself on a horse. I got a flying lesson. Fortunately about 75 percent of them don't mind a bit.**

When Jerry accidentally calls Pixel a he, Mark corrects him: **"I have friends who have a he, but I have a she."**

Mark is unruffled by Jerry's charges that his acts are immoral, illegal, and just plain gross, although he does admit he has had periods of self-doubt. **"Every time I've tried to deny my nature, it's been a train wreck. Since I accepted myself, I've been much happier."**

Their Happy Home

Jerry plays a video of a day in the life of Mark and Pixel. A ramp in front of their home allows Pixel easy access. Mark prepares pasta, which Pixel hungrily scarfs down from a plate set on a living room chair. A biscuit is passed from Mark's mouth to hers.

Mark describes their wedding ceremony. **"I knelt by her and held her hoof in my hand."** She looked at him towards the end of their vow exchange **"as if to say, 'It's about time you made me an honest woman.'"** Reminiscing with Pixel over a photo album, Mark spies a shot of Pixel in white panties (their wedding night?). He gushes lavishly about his love (see box on page 122), as if he's speaking about a human mate.

My Darling Pony

"What we have together is a romance. I feel honored to be able to share my life with her, have it returned. I enjoy looking at other horses, but she's mine, and I'm hers. Back in my early years, it was any mare I could get to. She was not an easy [bleep]. I had to earn her respect and her love. As far as sex goes, we make love. We don't fool around on each other. Sometimes we do have wild [bleep] and crazy sex. I'm not [bleep] like a horse, but that doesn't seem to matter to her. She still has her orgasms. We do just about everything human couples can do. I just wish we could have children. God I love her. God I love her. Thank God for her."

Relaxing at home.

Yes, that's their wedding album.

After you, dear.

Doggy-Style

After taking a much-needed break, Jerry introduces Rebecca and her "boyfriend" of 10 years, a canine named King. Rebecca sports an obvious blond wig and dark shades, and has requested that her voice be electronically disguised. Jerry plunges right in:

Jerry: **Do you understand you're not supposed to have sex with a dog?**

Rebecca: **A lot of people feel that way. It's something I've done for years.**

To Rebecca, sleeping with animals is **"an alternative lifestyle."** She says she has been with men during her life. **"Do they bark?"** Jerry cleverly inquires. But human relationships are **"not as gratifying emotionally or sexually."** to Rebecca.

She was a tender 13 when she first got aroused by noticing the genitals of the family's dog, and a couple of weeks later they had intercourse. **"That was painful the first time."**

Rebecca found her penchant for pooches so pronounced she once had an affair with the mutt of her live-in lover (she didn't consider that cheating!). Eventually he caught them in the act—whereupon he kicked Rebecca, broke her rib, and threw her out. And then he shot the dog.

Backstage Secrets—Revealed!

The call came under the request Do you have an alternative lifestyle? The message Mark left was short—but provocative: "I left my wife for a horse." Associate producer Toby Yoshimura figured this was a prank call, but he called back anyway.

At 6:30 the next morning Toby's home phone rang (producers forward their calls to their houses at night so they can be reached for emergencies). It was Mark. Toby was sure Mark was serious as he relayed his tale of, well, animal husbandry. But could Mark prove it? No problem; Mark soon showed explicit photos of himself engaged in numerous sex acts with his pony. He detailed the do's and don'ts, including using lot of lubricant and wearing a crash helmet. Through Mark, Toby quickly got in touch with other "zoos"—what people who sleep with animals prefer to be called——and soon dogs, goats, and sheeps were all guest possibilities.

Getting the animals to Chicago was a major obstacle, however. The man with the goats was thousands of miles away. The sheep guy wouldn't allow his animal to be shown on-camera. Another unusual behind-the-scenes moment came when producers contacted a fast-food chain to see if they could film Mark and Pixel in their typical run for french fries, but the restaurant balked.

Another Canine Cruiser

Apparently, Rebecca is far from alone in her attraction. Brad brings out his dog, Lady. **"We've been together four years. We go out for pizza, rent movies, camp."** And of course they have sex. Although Brad claims he has **"no feelings of guilt whatsoever,"** his need to come on the show disguised in a wig, beard, and glasses, and his visible nervousness say otherwise.

Brad's only sexual experience outside of animals was one gay relationship. Jerry inquires, **"Wouldn't you want to try a woman before a dog?"** While Brad may not, it seems that his dog might like to sample her own species: King and Lady nuzzle each other until they are pulled apart by their owners. (Lady has been with other dogs before, and has even had a litter.)

The Expert Psychologist

Springer "resident psychologist" Dr. Robert Butterworth, Ph.D., comes onstage and pronounces these people crazy. **"Let them run free,"** he urges the humans. He acknowledges that normal teens may sometimes wonder about such things, but this extreme example worries him: **"I'm afraid there are young people watching this, sitting home lonely, and they're looking at their pets in a new way."** Mark takes offense at Dr. Robert's charge that he is in love with a **"dumb animal."** Mark: **I'll give her an IQ test and she'll probably test out higher than half the audience.**
Dr. Butterworth: **Probably higher than you!**

What's It All About, Jerry?

"Surely this violates every Biblical, moral, and legal dictate on the matter. I mean, if this isn't sick, what is? We all love our pets, but to use an animal as a replacement for a human suggests an immediate visit to a doctor. You can love and admire the beauty and grace of a horse. You can pet it. You can even bet on it. But if you're going to ride it, make sure you're up in the saddle.

"Till next time, take care of yourself and each other."

Rebecca and King enjoying some "quality time."

Brad, with his Lady.

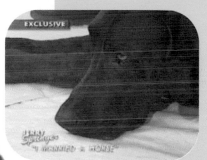

"Are you involved in a kinky relationship and want out? If so, call 1-800-96 JERRY."

"When other people go out and rent adult videos, do you rent *Mr. Ed?*"

What's in a Name?

There is an unmistakable art to the titling of each *Jerry Springer Show* episode—and after more than 1,400 shows, the producers refine this art more and more every day as they search for new and provocative ways of characterizing their explosive presentations. The following list presents hundreds of our favorite titles from over the years in chronological order, each one a dramatic encapsulation, an amusing declaration, or at the very least, a good title for a country and western song. Individual boxes highlight selected titles from frequent *Springer* topics.

Ethnic Dating Game
Crisis Makeovers
My Parents' Divorce Ruined My Life
When Jerry Met Sally (Jessy)
Raped, Tortured and Still Alive
My Kid Won't Stop Eating
I Gave Myself an Abortion
Do Fat People Make Better Lovers?
My Fiancé Won't Marry Me Until I Stop
    Stripping
Jerry Joins the Homeless
I Check the Mail 50 Times a Day
I Hate Going Outside to Smoke
They Stole My Husband's Eyes
I Woke Up in the Morgue
I Hit Rock Bottom, Now I'm on Top
Sneaking Around with a Black Man
I Love My Mother So Much, I'll Kill Her
The Lottery Will Send You to Hell
Pornography Destroyed My Life
That's No Woman, She's a He!
The Lord Has Ruined My Life
Men That Women Hate
I Left My Wife for Another Man
A Ghost Threw Me Down the Stairs
Topless Dancers and Their Sins
I Worshipped Satan at Age 6
Men Who Like Their Women Mean
Women Without Hair
Your Words Are Killing Me
I Have a Disease and the Doctors Won't Treat
    Me
Older Women and Younger Men
I Married a PMS Monster
Pregnant Women Need Not Apply
My Doctor Never Went to Med School
I Hate the Way My Sister Dresses
I'm Suing My Dad for Rape
I Sold My Baby
I Can't Get Over Elvis
Phone Sex Killed My Husband
My Therapist, My Lover
I'm Fat and I'm Proud
I Do Drugs at Church
Do-It-Yourself Abortions
Homosexual Cures
My Dad Wears Women's Clothing
Girls in the Gang
Nude Maids and Hot Dog Babes
I Hate Being Blond
Mother's Controlling My Life
Home Nudity

Klanning Around

Trying To Reason with Teens Who Want to Join the Klan

Honey, Please Don't Join the Klan

Christmas with the Klan

Klan TV

Klan Wedding

I'm A Breeder for The Klan

Pimps, Pimps, Pimps!

Teen Prostitutes and Pimps

My Brother's a Pimp

My Pimp Won't Let Me Go!

Prostitutes vs. Pimps

My Pimp Runs My Family

Ladies Who Steal
I Hate My Son's Long Hair
I'm Fighting for My Grandchildren
Gossip Almost Made Me Kill Myself
Dwarves Are People Too
Moms Addicted to Gambling
My Husband's a Fat Slob
I Didn't Know I Married a Rapist
I Hate Being Beautiful
I Spied on My Spouse
My Mother Flirts with Me
Big-Breasted Women
Making Love Behind Bars
Teen Vampires
Homosexual Boy Scouts
I Want My Daughter's Schoolbooks Banned
I Was Born a Boy and a Girl
Women Who Think Black Men Are No Good Part 1
Women Who Think Black Men Are No Good Part 2
Men Who Think They Know What Women Want
Help Me Stop Spoiling My Kids
I Live with a Nag
My Classmates Beat Me Up
I Can't Stop Lying
Porno Saved My Marriage
Beer, Broads, and TV: Real Life Al Bundys
Obnoxious Little League Parents
I Gave Birth to an Albino
From Nerd to Knockout
I Buy It, Wear It, and Take It Back
I'm Part of a Menage à Trois
My Parrot Runs My Life
We Lived a Wedding Day Nightmare
I'm Not the Family Maid
My 10-Year-Old Is an Atheist
Men Who Love Big-Bottomed Women
My Husband Doesn't Kiss Me Anymore
Sexual Fantasy Almost Ruined My Marriage
I'm Fat and Gay and Nobody Wants Me
Drag Queens and the People Who Love Them

White People Who Act Black
Adults Who Act Like Babies
I Used to Be Gorgeous and Now I'm Fat
I Molested My Daughter and She Forgave Me
Gays Raising Children
He Left Me Over Shopping
I Hate My Husband's Ex
99-Year-Old and His Young Lover
My 5-Year-Old Weighs 100 Pounds
I Can't Accept My Son as a Woman
They Call Me the Elephant Woman
Landlord from Hell
I Killed My Boyfriend Before He Killed Me
People Who Think They're Always Right
Guinness Book Losers
I Almost Lost My Kids Because They're Fat
Men Who Work in the Nude
I'm Mentally Disabled and Married
I Lost My Hair and I Lost My Job
My Brainwashed Husband Stole My Kids
Lesbians Shock Shoppers in the Mall
I'm Losing My Mind Over Menopause
Male Escorts Who Want Out
I Was Tricked into Marriage
Teen Transsexual
I'm Too Fat to Work
Deadly Erotic Teen Games
My Priest Betrayed Me
I Spent $55,000 to Look Like Barbie
Black Blondes
I Have Michael Jackson's Skin Disease
Hairy Women
I Caught My Peeping Tom
Having Affairs Saved Our Marriage
My Daughters and I Posed for *Playboy*
My 11-Year-Old is an Ordained Minister
Girl Boxer
Sisters Who Love Men in Prison
My Mom Is from Venus
I'm Ashamed of the Way My Son Treats Women
I Want to Buy a Bride for My Son
Couples Who Fist Fight
How to Survive Your Husband's Affair
Psychic Finds Missing People
Parents Upset Over Kid's Body Piercing
Moms Who Dress Pre-Schoolers Provocatively
Dads Who Hate Barney
Dads Afraid of Their Babies
Bodybuilder Adores Fat Women

Wacky Talk Show Guests: Why Do They Do It?
Male School Teacher Living As a Lesbian
I'm Jealous of My Wife's Weight Loss
Gorgeous Men Who Are Looking for Wives
Men and Women Who Beat Drums to Relieve Stress
My Son's Girlfriend Is Ruining His Life
Women Spend One Day as a Man
Gorgeous Men vs. Average Men: Who Do Women Prefer?
KKK Moms Take in Troubled Teens
Past Life Regression
How to Control Your Controlling Spouse
Kids Who Turn in Parents for Drug Use
I Look Just Like Oprah!
Parents Who Have Lost Control of Their Kids Fight Back
Trying to Reason with Teens Who Want to Join the Klan
Mississippi Violence Over Lesbian Camp
Should a Convict Get a New Heart?
Women Who Sell Their Babies
Fat Discrimination
Kids Who've Been Kicked Out Plead with Parents to Come Home
14 Year Old Girl Married Polygamist Man
My Teenage Daughter Is a Prostitute
I Got My Mom Off Crack
Senior Citizen Racists
Mad Dads

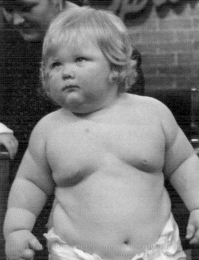

I'm Tired of Raising Another Woman's Children
My Daughter Was Beaten Up by Her Classmates Because She Is Beautiful
Men Who Don't Understand Their Overweight Wives
My Mom Is a Prostitute
Moms Confront the Neo-Nazi They Claim Brainwashed Their Kids
Young Chauvinists Defend Their Sexist Attitudes
Mom's Punk Rock Career Is More Important Than Her Daughter
I'm Too Fat to Get Out of Bed
Peach County, Georgia, Mad Over Nude Diner
7- and 9-Year-Old Sisters Want to Join the KKK
I Hate My Daughter's Boyfriend
Boy Wants to Be a Girl
I Slept with My Wife's Sister
Housewives Become Strippers
My Husband Stole My Kids
Transsexual Beauty Pageant
14-Year-Old Girl and Her 1,600-Pound Mom
17-Year-Old Marries 71-Year-Old
My Girlfriend and My Ex Are Best Friends
My Moustache Is 8 Feet Wide...and Other Unusual Stories
Teen Prostitutes and Pimps
My Daughter Wants to Be a Man
Stripper Siblings
I Became a Stripper Because Mom

Abandoned Me
Fat Man Pageant
Gangs Invade Suburbia
I Had an Affair Because My Husband Neglected Me
I Caught My Husband Having an Affair with My Aunt
Girls in Gangs
Fat Greeting Card Models
I Don't Agree with My Daughter's Lifestyle
My Husband Doesn't Think I'm Sexy
Parents Reunited with the Children They Gave Up
My Husband Became a Woman
Women Tired of Being Seen as Sexual Objects
Our Father Is a Monster
I Hate My Best Friend
Skinhead Romances
Am I a Boy or a Girl?
Beauty Pageant for Pregnant Women
I Married a Slob
Dancing Made Me Hate Men
Help! I Need More Romance
I Hate My Daughter's Body Piercing
Couples Make Fantasy Home Video
Mom Acts Like a Teenager
My Daughter Wants to Be an Adult Film Actress
Why'd You Dump Me?
Is Breast Size Important?
I'm Embarrassed by My Friend's Weight
I Make My Living in Bikini Contests
I'm Dating a Loser
I'm in Love with a Jerry Springer Guest
I Strip with My Family
I'm Raising My Daughter to Hate Men
The Woman I Love Is a Man
Love Me My Way or No Way
Honey, Please Don't Join the Klan
My Boyfriend Turned Out to Be a Girl
My Wife Is a Tease
College Kids in the Sex Industry
My Best Friend Steals My Dates
I Want a Pure Woman
I Want to Quit My Job for a Sexy Career
I Hate My Wife's Gay Friend
Don't Marry That Jerk
High-class Hookers Tell All
I Hate My Best Friend's Lover
I'm Not the Man I Used to Be
I Want to Model for Adult Magazines
I'm Kicking My Roommate Out!
My Boyfriend Is a Male Escort
My Best Friend Is a Back-stabber

I'm Furious That You're Gay!
Best Friends Compete for the Same Lover
Secret Crushes: Gay on Straight
Catfighters
Honey, Have I Got a Secret for You!
Pregnant Bad Girls
My Roommate Steals My Men
My Girlfriend Is a Man
I Hate My Lover's Promiscuous Past
I'll Do Anything to Kill Your Relationship
My Sister Is Too Wild
A Gay Wedding
My Lover Is a Cheating Dog
My Girlfriend Is a Call Girl
I'm Marrying My Uncle
Abandoned at the Altar
My Friend Stole My Girlfriend
I'm Proud to Be a Virgin
Mom's Man Is a Loser
I Want a Threesome
Dump That Third Wheel
I Can't Forgive You for What You Did
Female Impersonators
Bachelorette Party Fights
Gays of Our Lives
I Want to Confront My Ex
My Man Is a Dog
Why'd You Leave Me?
Help! I Slept with My Best Friend
We're All in Love with the Same Person

Weighty Matters

Do Fat People Make Better Lovers?

I'm Fat and I'm Proud

I'm Fat and Gay and Nobody Wants Me

My Husband's a Fat Slob

I'm Too Fat to Get Out of Bed

I'm Too Fat to Work

Fat Man Pageant

Fat Greeting Card Models

You're Too Fat to Dress Like That

You're Too Fat to Make Porn

14-Year-Old Girl and Her 1,600-Pound Mom

600-Pound Angry Mom

What Did You Expect?

Beauty Pageant for Pregnant Women

Pregnant Bad Girls

I'm a Pregnant Prostitute

Pregnant and Tormented

My Sister Is Pregnant by My Ex

Pregnant and Dumped

I'm Seven Months Pregnant and Still Stripping

I'm Pregnant and Have to Strip

I'm Pregnant by My Kidnapper

I'm Pregnant...Stop Cheating!

I Want Someone I Can't Have
Grow Up Already! You Look Like a Freak
Get Your Mitts Off My Man
My Partner Can't Get Enough
Stop Your Wild Ways
My Lover Is Lazy...in Bed!
My Lover Is a Strip Club Junkie
The Great Mate Swap
I Want Revenge for What You Did
I'll Do Anything for One Night with You
Girl, I Need a New Look!
I Hate My Twin's Lover
You're Too Sexy for Your Own Good
You're Ruining Our Relationship
We Seduce Women for Points
Warning: My Ex Is a Jerk
Got Caught Cheating
I Could Steal Your Man in a Minute
My Best Friend Is Ruining My Life
Stay with Your Own Race
You've Turned My Life into a Soap Opera
A Woman Wants My Boyfriend
You Promised You'd Stop
Stop Interfering in My Relationship
One Woman Isn't Enough
My Girlfriend Is a Gold-Digger
My Dad Is a Woman
I'll Do Anything to Break You Up
I Was Dumped on the *Springer Show*
My Husband Had a Sex Change
Stop the Wedding!
Interracial Secret Crushes
You're Ruining Our Family Name
Get Over Me Already!
I Hate Your Relationship
Sexy Twins

You're a Cradle Robber
I Can Get Anyone I Want
The Wedding's Off
Personal Ad Nightmares
I Do...I Don't
My Wife's Sleeping with My Aunt
I Want to Be an Escort
I'm Having Your Man's Baby
Stop Selling Your Body
I'm Better for You
We Compete for Dates
I Regret We Met
Your Lover Is a Loser
Confess, You Liar
You Used Me
Dump That Cheater
Black Sheep of the Family
Date Swap
I Can't Stand My Sibling
Why Are You in a Gang?
You Could do Better
I Can't Forgive You
Psychics at the Scene
Bizarre Love Triangles
Surprise Proposals
I'm Both a Man and a Woman
I Have Six Wives
I'm a Pregnant Prostitute
You Make My Life Miserable
Dumped!
You're Making a Mistake
Stay Out of Our Lives
I'm Stuck in a Love Triangle
I've Got a Secret Crush on You
Pregnant and Tormented
Wives Confront Cheating Husbands
Back Off My Lover
Butt Out!
Extreme Fighting
My Family Locked Me Up
Stop Selling Sex
I Have 15 Personalities
Real-Life Soap Operas
Klan TV
It's Time You Found Out
My Man Wears a Dress
We Live in a Car
My Wife and I Have the Same Lover
Ex-Lovers in Crises
You're Eating Yourself to Death
Trust Me, I've Changed
My Mom Sold Us
Klan Wedding
Real Life X-Files
We Still Live in a Car
This Is Your Last Chance
I Live as the Opposite Sex
I Weigh 700 Pounds
Mom Loves You More
You Were Never a Mother
You Disgust Me
Mom, How Could You Do This?
Zack...The 70-Pound Baby
My Wife Weighs 900 Pounds

My Marriage is a Mistake
Why Are You Together?
Your Ex Is Breaking Us Up
I'm Sorry, I Cheated
I'm Jealous of My Gay Friend
That Man Will Ruin You!
I Can't Stop Dating Convicts
Female Chain Gang
My 15-Year-Old Son Wears a Dress
I'm in Love with a Serial Killer
The Man with Eight Wives
We're in Holiday Hell!
Do You Still Want Me...or Her?
I Still Love My Ex
I Want Out of This Threesome
My Wife Wants to Be a Call Girl
Why I Sell My Body
Teenage Drag Queens
I'm Making My First Adult Film
It's Your Baby...and I Have Proof
Close That Strip Club Down!
My Girlfriend's a Guy
That Man's No Good
I'm Having Your Husband's Baby
I Had a Sex Change at 50 Years Old
Surprise...I Slept with Your Man
Your Lifestyle Will Ruin Us
We Just Fulfilled Our Fantasy
My Fiancé Wants Me to Be a Racist
My Sister Is Pregnant by My Ex
I'm 16 and My Husband Is 36!
I'm Here to Break You Up
Male Siamese Twins
Pregnant and Dumped
Stop Stalking My Man
I'm a Breeder for The Klan

My Brother's a Pimp
Wild Ways to Make a Living
I Want to Be a Centerfold
My Sister Stole My Husband
I'm Seven Months Pregnant and
    Still Stripping
Stop Selling Your Body
I Hate My Girlfriend's Sexy Job
I Know You're Cheating!
My Girlfriend Is Really a Man!
Dumped on *Springer*
I Want to Strip for My Man
You're Better Off Single!
You'll Never Marry Our Daughter
I'm Marrying a Transsexual
I'm Here to Dump You
Be Honest...Are You Cheating?
Choose Me or Lose Me
I'm Sleeping with Your Man
Surprise...Meet My New Lover
Paternity Tests Revealed
I Broke the World's Sex Record
KKK Parents
It's Your Bachelor Party or Me
Adult Film Stars Tell All
I've Been Keeping a Secret
I Can't Let You Get Married
You're Too Fat to Dress Like That
I'm Proud to Be a Racist
My Sister Ruined My Life
I Have a Secret...I'm a Call Girl!
My Teen Worships Satan
Surprise! I Have a Bisexual Lover
I'm Pregnant by My Kidnapper
You're a Home-wrecker!
My Girlfriend Is a Cheater!
A Teenager's Pregnant with My
    Man's Baby
Wife Discovers Husband's Secret
    Family
Quit The Klan!
I'm Pregnant...Stop Cheating!
Paternity Results: I Slept with Two
    Brothers!

My Pimp Won't Let Me Go!
Why'd You Cheat?
Honey, I'm Really a Guy!
Pregnant Bad Girls
You Dumped Me at the Altar!
It's Either Me or Her!
I Refuse to Wear Clothes!
I Will Break You Up!
Who's the Father of My Baby?
My Niece Stole My Husband
I'm Pregnant and Have to Strip
I Can't Stay Faithful
I'm Here to Stop Your Wedding!
Leave That Loser!
This Is Our Nice Holiday Show
Jerry Rescues a 1,200-Pound
    Couple
Teenage Call Girls
You Have One More Chance!
Dump Your Lover...You're Mine!
It's Your Mother or Me!
I'm Married but Live with My Lover
Stripper Wars
I Have Too Many Lovers!
I Have Sex with My Sister
Past Guests Attack!
Home-wreckers Confronted!
Honey...I'm a Call Girl!
I'm Having a Bisexual Affair
I Won't Let You Sell Your Body
Guess What?...I'm a Man!
I've Had Enough...It's Over!
Get Your Own Man!
Prostitutes vs. Pimps
I'm Here to Divorce You!
Adult Babies
Attack of the Ex-Lovers
I Share My Lover!
Why Did We Marry? You're Gay!
I'm Here to Confront My One Night
    Stand!
It's Time to Choose!
Mistresses Attack
My Pimp Runs My Family

My Uncle Stole My Wife
Like It or Not, I'm Pregnant!
600-Pound Angry Mom
Stripper Love Triangles
Butt Out of Our Threesome!
You're a Man...Dress Like One!
You're Too Fat to Make Porn
My Granny Robbed the Cradle
I'll Do Anything to Break You Up
It's Over but I Still Want You!
I'll Make a Choice Today
I'm Not a Home-wrecker—You Are!
Mom, Will You Marry Me?
Confronting Home-Wreckers
You'd Better Choose Me!
My Wife Left Me for My Father
Wives and Mistresses Do Battle!
I'm Taking Your Man!
I'm Lying to My Lover
Stay Out of My Threesome!
I Stole My Mom's Man!
Lesbian Cousins in Love
Attack of the Angry Wives
In-Laws Face Off
I Watched My Lover Have Sex with
    4 Men
My Mother Made Me a Prostitute
My Race Is Best
Shocking Truths Exposed!
Sizzling Lesbian Sex Scandals
I Love Being Naked!